Living in a
ZIGZAG
Age

Living in a
ZIGZAG
Age

Bryant M. Kirkland

Abingdon Press
Nashville-New York

LIVING IN A ZIGZAG AGE

Copyright © 1972 by Abingdon Press

ISBN 0-687-22403-9

Library of Congress Catalog Card Number: 79-173950

MANUFACTURED BY THE PARTHENON PRESS AT
NASHVILLE, TENNESSEE, UNITED STATES OF AMERICA

To My Father
Henry Burnham Kirkland

PREFACE

This book was written for those who are not yet thirty years old and face the opportunity of several mid-course corrections in their life plans. It was also written for those past thirty who now sense, even more keenly, that their personal needs and styles change more swiftly than they did formerly. Life drifts out of focus unnoticeably, even as satellites vanish from the field of an astronomer's telescope and need constantly to be relocated. In each lifetime there are critical periods when one's life can be brought back into a sharper focus of both service and enjoyment.

Such refocusing of life can be much more than a helpful change of life style or a deeper, personal spiritual adjustment. It can mean a stimulating shift in perspective or a change of vocation. Now, more than years ago, modern men and women can plan for basic changes in their lives, in education, in service, and in retirement. Besides, there are increasing opportunities to achieve upward mobility from the bondage of poverty or one of the minority groups.

No one needs to serve out his years as a prisoner without hope, because Christ came to give life abundant in this world as well as beyond it. To be able to refocus one's life from one period to the next, as well as to help others to do it, is part of the Christian adventure. The key idea in this book is that life under God is a process involving change and growth.

I am especially appreciative of the helpfulness of Mrs. Grace Schneider, my research and editorial assistant, who not only typed the entire manuscript through several revisions but provided helpful spiritual insights and technical counsel as well.

During the months of writing I have been grateful for the understanding of my wife, Bernice Tanis Kirkland, and our daughters' families. In fact, the more one refocuses his life, the more he realizes how much he owes to so many—his family, colleagues, dear friends, and that unknown company who walk the same daily pathway.

This book is sent forth with the hope that many can start fresh chapters in their lives and that all of us can help younger people to achieve what God desires to give them in the creative years ahead.

BRYANT M. KIRKLAND

The Fifth Avenue Presbyterian Church
New York

CONTENTS

I. You Have to Run to Stay Where You Are

Keeping Life in Focus— against a shifting background

It is not true that all that is in the effect appears in the cause.
—*Jules Simon*

One has only to stand still to get lost in life. Traffic swirls about him as in Piccadilly Circus or Times Square. Routes and airline schedules may be changed without any obligation of notice. Weather, without consideration, closes in with its mantle of fog, and by its closure people lose days that they may never regain.

Youths change radically over ten years, as do older men and women in more subtle ways. Customs alter swiftly now because cultural conditions vary with technology and affluence. Revolutions today are not always as explosive as was the destruction of the Bastille. Hence, no one can remain the same in turbulent life, for just to try to do so accelerates the shifting conditions of life for other people who are put under pressure to adjust to another's unadjusting. In other words, life is made up of change.

The continuing motion of circumstances and people's choices make it essential to personality to keep putting life back into focus—not so much back into focus just as it was but moving into clearer focus on whatever now is the scene. By continually adjusting to the sharp focus of life, one maintains his vitality and sense of adventure. On the other hand, to permit life's focus to fade or blur only increases the burden of boredom and resignation. But apathy and despair are not contributive to personal development, nor are they elements in the catalog of spiritual graces taught by Christ.

Paul recognized the problem modern people face in their turbulence when he wrote, "Now we see through a glass, darkly; . . . but then shall I know even as also I am known" (I Cor. 13:12).

I

Few people are born with an adequate tradition or system of thought sufficient to carry them through the years of cyclical change or the cyclonic developments of technology. It used to be possible to fulfill one's years within the same cohesive system of ideas and values as one's parents. Today, one's value system must be reappraised and personally appropriated afresh if it is to be useful, or appreciated, or helpful.

Actually, each generation has had to follow this same process, but in other eras changes were gradual and often imperceptible until they reached a cataclysm and burst into a recognizable new period of life-style.

The cities and art galleries of Europe witness to this series of gradual and radical changes and their aftermath. What were once proud designs of Greek or Roman pagan temples, often the scenes of licentious rites, were changed to become the models of architecture for dynamic Christianity in its renewing sweep across the West. The old way was renovated for the new focus of faith and purposive direction of service.

Only a short walking tour through the Louvre reveals the same history of change in painting and sculpture. Greek and Roman statues of gods made in the image of heroic men yielded to the artistic brushwork of painters who idealized the biblical stories and virtues in the cultural patterns of their own respective ages. However, when the world did not come to an end in the year A.D. 1000 as had been predicted, artists started moving more swiftly toward a new focus of reality and humanity. Instead of angels on clouds and sad men afraid of portentous doom, they painted men who had a new optimism about life's worthwhile meanings.

Painters saw more of the dignity and the glory of God in his creatures' faces than in a cherub's countenance. The title of a painting, "A Man," was sufficient to describe the dignity of a person without a name.

But even the Renaissance man's rediscovery of life drifted out of focus after its fresh start. Habitude and familiarity plus conventionalism and indolence made a repetitious style of it. The vigor and clarity and newness were gone. Charity often calls the peak of such previous models classical when they have passed their zenith. Unkindly and unperceiving critics often label the emergent new style radical or barbaric, even when it contains the basis for seeking a new focus. In fact, the criticism and the creative correction both need each other for new insights.

One can see the emergence of brilliant light values and fresh interpretations of reality in the collection of modern painters of the French School on exhibition at Jeu de Paume, a part of the Louvre, in the corner where the Rue de Rivoli spills speeding traffic into the Place de la Concorde. There, near the ancient obelisk of Egypt, telling in hieroglyphics of past glories, are the brilliant colors of the impressionistic painters of France. There one can see the trend begun in the middle of the nineteenth century. Modern art came quietly long before the jazz era, just as all changes of life-style usually have earlier roots.

The Impressionist school of painting began when Edgar Degas (1834-1917) saw the pain and glory of life fresh in every scene, in every common face. He gave realism to background with depth and details. Life could not be a pose like a portrait. For him it had to include the influence of circumstances and surroundings. Nor were all his paintings those of gracious ladies with wealthy husbands to pay for their elegances. In 1876, Degas caught the tragic loneliness of a man and a woman seated at an outdoor cafe. The simple title, "L'absinthe," tells the pathetic story marked in the dejection of their lips and the upturn of their worn shoes showing on the flagstones under the table.

From then on other painters saw more light and humanity in nature, and men like Renoir, Monet, Cézanne, Pissarro, and Manet, not forgetting the tragic Dutch minister's son Vincent Van Gogh, began to paint realistically in a new focus.

Turner, the British painter of light, declared the doctrine that each one had to break with tradition and create new arrangements. That sounds like heresy in religion and radicalism in a world that often would rather legislate conformity than expend the energy required for a new birth and a clearer focus of life.

Yet it was Christ's insistence on a new focus in all the realms of society that created his jeopardy and provoked his crucifixion. But today we have stylized Christianity again so that it is often safer to conform to its ecclesiastical and cultural configurations than to apply creatively the dynamics of its Founder. In truth it is risky, to individuals as well as to institutions, to entertain even the thought that Christ might again put some new things in fresh focus as he did when he first came.

14

Do you remember how angry the citizens became when the Lord pointed out to them that they were more interested in their donkey in the ditch than in the man fallen by the gutter? His whole point was one of focus, not whether donkeys or men or sparrows were of more or less value, but that it takes focus to know the difference in varied circumstances. Since upsetting changes come even to those who do nothing, and even their immobility makes others change, then each of us needs to learn how to bring life into focus when it drifts away again.

II

Change is part of redemption—to use the churchly word that stands for personal renewal of life and the refocusing of purpose and values. Without change there can be no real renewal. However, that change may often be painful or severe.

It was that way for the *Mayflower* Pilgrims when they fled to the hospitality of Holland before coming to the American wilderness. The 350th anniversary of their courageous voyage, commemorated in 1970, marked a good opportunity for everyone to begin a new decade of life and ministry with an examination of his life's course and any required refocusing of values and purposes. My return trip to England, Holland, and France, where these chapters are being written, had provided stimulus to personal pursuit of a renewed spiritual focus for daily life and for new skills to meet the contemporary challenges to Christ's church. Sometimes one has to leave the country in order to gain a fresh insight into home. More often he has to learn how to work out renewal on the street where he lives with all its familiar demands for continuity rather than for refocusing.

On any boulevard there are men and women finding God and losing him at the same time on the same spot. They may be seated quietly at the same sidewalk cafe in the Montparnasse district or lost in deep thought of new aspirations or of old regrets, because Paris can reveal life or death, but so can New York or Ponca City. The place does not bring out the focus. It is the lens of the soul, not the scene, which changes. But strange faces and words can force the soul's attention quicker than can the preoccupation of the familiar setting of home communities.

An angry woman with a drawn face just screamed above the traffic at a passing gendarme. Her cry was abusive and shrill. She needed more help than the police could afford. Curious eyes, some tender, others laughing in self-protectiveness, looked intently at what years of inner torment had done to her. Was it too late for a new focus to come to her aggravated emotional life? Perhaps not, if one would take the patience to quench the hostility and relieve the fear that raged within her mind. No doubt there had been earlier times when refocusing her life would have been easier, but she had continued on her driven way without change, relief, or redirection.

One can hope it will be much easier for the American boy who was murmuring to himself, walking near the Place de la Madeleine. In passing, it seemed as if the love of his life had disappointed him, and he was trying to work it out to a new focus in his own language in a strange land.

Thomas Wolfe wrote poignantly that you can't go home again. Unfortunately, many feel that this is true. But the Christian gospel is borne out by history that a person can always find new focus, can always arise and go home, can discover a new personal life or create a new thoroughfare for freedom's sake. There is always a new turn possible on even the hardest road, and there is always a gate in the thorniest hedge.

The Hollanders were hosts to the *Mayflower* Pilgrims in their long search for a new life. The Dutch have always been liberal toward seekers after truth. Perhaps their relentless labors to keep their land standing dry above the waters of the sea have made them patient and tolerant of hardship.

They did not forget their hospitality or freedom when the Nazis persecuted the Jews in Holland during World War II. A visit to the home of Anne Frank at 263 Prinsengracht, Amsterdam, stirs one's soul intensely; for it was there that the pages of her adolescent diary were discovered in a back room after the Gestapo had arrested the family and ransacked the place, leaving the scrawled pages of her record of exile behind.

Today, one can enter the secret quarters where faithful friends hid the Frank family. One swings open the same large, hinged bookcase that hid their secret door and then climbs up a steep stair, like a ship's ladder, to see the lines they penciled on the wallpaper to mark the growth of the children; while similarly on a war map pasted to the wall next to the markings, they moved colored pins to show the progress of hoped-for deliverance by the advancing Allied armies. Unfortunately, in August, 1944, someone betrayed them, and all were killed at Auschwitz except the father, who escaped from the camp. Today, the house stands just as the day it was raided, to remind all people that individual men and women can live with high purpose in the worst of times, and in the best of times they must keep refocusing their lives on the everlasting principles of Christian living by discovering fresh and new insights of vital application.

If the Hollanders had been content to remember only their earlier help to the Pilgrims, they would have been blind to the refocus of their own faith in the twentieth century when they helped the persecuted Jews and so demonstrated that all individuals as well as social institutions, in every changeful decade, need to refocus themselves to new values and pur-

17

poses created by kaleidoscopic forces and intrusive circumstances beyond anyone's control.

III

It is necessary to refocus life to live effectively. Life is
continual but not continuous. That is its challenge to ingenuity, creativity, and character. There are backward steps and
side steps to ordered progress. There are typhoons and cy-
clones besides the fair winds of steady sailing. A person may
move creatively through ten or twenty years and then come
to a standstill for one, or five, or even ten years more. Even
that, however, need not be the end of his creative usefulness
if he will refocus his life. The adjustment may be a radical
one, but the results may be amazingly productive—like the
time that Winston Churchill was defeated in office after World
War II by an impatient and weary electorate. A lesser man
might have retired to his estate in Kent and lived out the end
of his seventy or eighty years amidst old mementos of former
triumphs, but Sir Winston refocused his life in the defeat
and the strident challenge of postwar society to come back
to an even more illustrious leadership. He made a demonstration of personal tenacity at a trying period in his own
life's course, when so many other men and women falter in the
middle of a career or near its end. That is why the green
onyx tablet set in the flagstone floor of Westminster Abbey
says so boldly and helpfully, "Remember Winston Churchill."

In the strange optimism of American life, schoolchildren
learn a myth of continuous onward progress. The many his-
torical wounds of European life remind even the sanguine
that life has its paradoxes, its reversals as well as its surges of
progress. The eminent Swiss psychiatrist Paul Tournier
pointed out so helpfully that there are no absolute successes or
failures. It is what a person does to refocus even his successes
as well as his failures toward a continuing direction of life

under God that counts most. Samuel Smiles wrote, "We often discover what will do by finding out what will not do; and probably those who never made a mistake never made a discovery."

In photography one usually focuses the sharpest image by bracketing a little over and a little under until the picture leaps into clarity. How helpful this truth would be if it were learned in youth as well as in the middle or late years. Would its awareness destroy the optimism of young people? No, it probably would develop even more freedom in them to be creative, to take initiative, to run risks, because in the end one must learn to cope with failure and disappointment as well as with achievement by refocusing his life from year to year.

IV

Life is exploratory at its best. History instructs life by showing in art and architecture the records of other men's readjustments to political forces, ambitions, plagues, wars, and poverty; but each person must write his own history of adjustment in the companionship of his own generation and in the terms of the duress of his own times. Reinhold Niebuhr reminded all that some of the facts of history are revocable if challenged with sufficient initiative, though irrevocable if accepted with complacency.

One's interpretation of his own life has to be validated by each day's testing in the particular milieu of one's own familiar surroundings of uncertainty. More than political premiers have been cast out of office by the electors' circumstances or whims. There are competitors in every art and science. The wild rains beat down the growing corn in the fields. Unexpected responsibilities are thrust on junior executives or young parents for which they have not prepared. Aged parents must often adjust to living in the family of their children. Even a grandfather must find sufficient added energy and patience to support his son's or daughter's broken family when he had thought he had earned a quiet life in a tidy house. No matter how much he loves them, it is an adjustment of magnitude.

Process is more descriptive of human existence than progress. Process includes the fall of autumn leaves, some into nourishing humus and others into acrid smoke and fire, as well as the springtime burst of bud, blossom, and leaf. Process involves sleep, illness, the broken leg suspended in traction, as well as the elegant swift flight of the snow skier, the driven middle-aged person at his confining task, or the exhaustion of the young after unrelieved gaiety. Not even a brick wall knows only stability and progress. The wind and rain beat upon it. Moss and flowers grasp it in gentle fingers, clutching at its mortared joints. Trucks or even donkeys brush their heavy burdens as pressures against the wall. Even stone walls need nurture and repair or they fall—but not in a sudden moment. How much more so is this true of modern men and women, particularly the stronger ones living under pressure.

V

But God has given basic skills to face the continuous work of refocusing or readjustment. Just to have the awareness of the need to adjust is to destroy the illusive myth of continuing progress and growth. To understand that even God pursues a zigzag course, rather than moving in a perfectly straight line, should be something of a helpful revelation.

Once God spoke in tones reminiscent of the Old Testament thunder. Then he spoke in the wooing words and characteristics of the life of Jesus Christ. In these latter days of the Holy Spirit's presence, he speaks in many different ways to win and assist people. If it were an easier way, there would not be the treasure of his many splendid ways of reaching diverse personalities who are trapped in their own ingenious obstinacies. If God himself can use the forbearance of process with its zigzag motion, its ups and downs of positive and negative steps, so can we. In fact, it is a superior skill to be able to change and refocus, as much so as flying an airplane is more difficult than driving a switchyard railroad engine, when even that locomotive could get derailed by the whimsy of an electric switch's malfunction.

Moreover, trustful obedience to the whole of life's forces and powers, as experienced over the ages, helps one to adjust to life. Normally we all try to force issues to our own conclusions, to frame up tidy programs which will not be subject to the inconvenience of change. But this is to ignore the possibility of faith and risk in every situation. Ultimately in each job, in every marriage, in all fashioning of personalities, one must take the leap of faith into creative uncertainty.

This is breathtakingly visible when the circus comes to town. Despite the ascending pitch of the band's music and the organ tones of the ringmaster's oratory generating excitement, one's own heart leaps too when the trapeze artist swings his lithe body into the arc of a triple somersault and is caught in the outstretched hands of his partner, who has timed his own rhythm to the other's. Is living a human life or following the spiritual path to God any less risky or less involving of trustful obedience? Sooner or later everyone will need to learn the deeper skill of trusting as much as he has depended on rigidity of attitude and rigorous planning.

The Bible points out still another way to refocus life besides those of recognizing the blessings of change and learning how to trust God, other people, and the swinging tides in the affairs of men. That other way is the one of abandonment. To leave a position, to change a custom or a prejudice, to confirm the futility of a situation is difficult for most people to do. Most of us remember the patriot's words, "Don't give up the ship," more than we recall the scriptural injunction to

Abraham, "Get thee out of thy country, and from thy kin-
dred, and from thy father's house, unto a land that I will
show thee" (Gen. 12:1). Then, too, there are the even more
practical words of the Savior, "Whosoever shall not receive
you, nor hear your words, when ye depart out of that house
or city, shake off the dust of your feet" (Matt. 10:14).

VI

The great American preacher Phillips Brooks started out
to be a teacher. He was chagrined at his failure in this chosen
career. But he was not too proud to refocus his life and yield
it to God's usefulness as a greater preacher and hymn writer.

It is not easy to accept limitations and disappointments.
But there are few useful and creative lives without them.
Usually the more significant patterns of service include a
generous portion of pain, bewilderment, and regret, to say
nothing of despair as the parent of ingenuity and discovery.

Today we idealize the name of Florence Nightingale, the
founder of modern nursing practice. But we must remember
she faced obdurate and malicious obstacles in ministering to
the wounds of men on the battlefield and in promoting their
healing in the hospitals of London in her own day. At the
present time the facilities of St. Thomas Hospital on the
Thames is a monument to her struggle. There where she
served, today the swinging cranes of modern construction
workers are adding new facilities, because even Florence
Nightingale's world of nursing has been changed with new
drugs, new human injuries and diseases, modern nuclear medicine, and advanced surgical skills. She, who once refocused
nursing service, may see her own courageous advances still
being brought up to date by refocusing.

Life's setbacks are not always destructive. They are a re-
versal of one's hopes, aims, and objectives, but they may be
a corrective or a supplement or even a new discovery. Just

as there are stages in the life cycle of development of most plants and animals, so man can learn that this applies also to him and even to God. This truth can be a radical discovery to a person, for there are lean seasons as well as fat ones in the soul's career. The Bible says, "To every thing there is a season, and a time to every purpose under the heaven: A time to be born, and a time to die; a time to plant, and a time to pluck up that which is planted; . . . a time to weep, and a time to laugh; a time to mourn, and a time to dance; . . . a time to get, and a time to lose; a time to keep, and a time to cast away" (Eccles. 3:1-6). A wise man senses that his seemingly wasted years in the desert may be the ones of his greatest training or development. In God's program, refocusing life synergizes both the good and the bad, the successes and the failures, for the glory of God's own purposes and for the enrichment of every individual who by Christ's grace can see the power of this truth.

One might refer here, for an example, to ancient Moses or to blind Louis Braille, the inventor of braille script, not to mention the stony path of great political leaders, including that of Richard M. Nixon and his crisis of leadership which he has weathered with tenacity and dedication.

Mistakes and their corrections are part of the artistry of life. The stone which the builders rejected may become the head of the arch. The lights of a painting create their own shadows. The detours of gravel roads and choking dust may be the shortest way back to the main highway. Therefore, it is wise to probe the limits of the place and time where one is. Few persons realize the depths and potentials of their present situation. We are always chagrined that someone else has seen more in a given environment than we discovered. What he has evolved out of it, we too could have developed if we had refocused our outlook, our attitudes, and our imagination.

To do this is not easy, nor is it possible to do so every time. There are occasions when one can only stand his ground and wait for the howling sandstorm to stop lacerating the tent collapsed over his head. There are other times when wisdom commands the navigator to strike the sails and let the storm blow him out to sea rather than to crush the hull on a rocky coast. One can always shake the sand from his hair after a desert storm, just as by the next day's light one can sail over the hissing billows toward a safe harbor. There is a time to win and a time to lose in life, and both are part of refocusing, although neither one is easy. But the failure to acknowledge the change in wind or sky can be fatal to the traveler on life's way. There are slow tides in the personal affairs of life that make one wait, and others that course at full speed. Waiting for God's favorable insights is just as useful as is feverish work when the signals are clear.

Refocusing life on Christ each day can lead to new discoveries amid familiar, if not congenial, circumstances. One prime goal may lead on and give the way to a secondary goal of even greater importance, as when penicillin was discovered inadvertently, just as was cortizone. The potentiality of fulfilling life lies more in refocusing everyday events and circumstances than it does in dreaming or fantasizing. The way a person journeys in life is often as important as the goal he seeks. Pioneers in the Bible all died without reaching their full hopes, but they left us a rich heritage of how to refocus each day's situation toward the main goal, to love and serve God sincerely within the situation at hand. This does not mean passive capitulation to one's lot in life. Rather, it means the harder the circumstances, the more one needs to refocus on Christ's spirit for the main direction for one's life, in order to make creative sense out of the present predicament.

A French metropolitan magazine spread these words on its recent cover: "Life is too short to tolerate without refocusing what appears to be mediocre." It takes courage to refocus one's life, but most people need what the Space Age calls frequent mid-course corrections in the orbit of one's flight plan.

Even while I am writing this chapter, the darkness has come and it has started to rain under a chill wind. But that change will make the hot tea and turnips at dinner taste better tonight, and there is also the promise of a good tomorrow. The complex of events and attitudes which constitute human existence represent "a bewildering confusion of destiny and freedom," * success and failure, which conform to no set pattern of logic or coherence. Rather, they find their unity by our daily refocusing them in faith toward the greater providence of God, who loves us and helps those who call upon him.

Who would have realized that a dozen years of imprisonment in Bedford jail for the sake of conscience would have engendered John Bunyan's richest contribution to many lives by his writing *The Pilgrim's Progress,* with its realistic account of man's painful trudge to victory through the Slough of Despond and up the Hill of Difficulty? Perhaps at the time even he did not realize you can live your life all over again with each new day's dawning and the renewed opportunity to refocus it on him who is both its beginning and its fulfillment.

* Reinhold Niebuhr, *Faith and History* (New York: Charles Scribner's Sons, 1949), p. 20.

You Can Live Life Over Again— but today is all you really have

With God, life is one and timeless. Only man uses clocks and calendars to measure his existence. They can be a blessing in marking the infinite succession of fresh beginnings granted unto man to live his life over again, or they can record his wasted hours. Of course, the days are connected to one another even though each is a fresh start. There are happy memories as well as unbalanced ledgers and traffic tickets. But there is each day's fresh vision and new energy to tackle the problems carried over. In this sense each day is a new chapter, because there can be a new focus and a renewal of wisdom to confront the ever-changing situation.

A person cannot hope to be reincarnated any more than he can dolefully wish for nonexistence—to cite two extreme ways people use to try to solve life's pain and problems. One can, however, gratefully receive the gift of each new day as a fresh beginning within the limits of his total years. People may motor through Bedford, England, in a swaying bus and nod as the tour director declares, "There is a statue of John

27

Bunyan on the village green." But the sharp pressure of hydraulic brakes at a near collision at the crossroads could drive away the memory of that ancient pilgrim of liberty. What really counts is that there are modern men and women languishing in jail now for the sake of conscience on several points, and we do not even know their names. Someday others who reap the benefits of their sacrifices will recognize them. In time, these names too will become tourists' items on a jolting itinerary while still new unknown persons continue to pay the price of suffering, while they claim the hope of a better world. You, too, can live your life over again each day, despite unhandy circumstances, if you focus it on a grand enough vision of God's kingdom's steady march beyond your own life-span.

Some people put their hope of the renewal of their lives in the new physiological methods of behavioral changes by chemistry or even cranial surgery. Even more people are acquainted with helpful psychological principles which lead toward better life adjustment, with increased productivity and a heightened sense of well-being.

Most individuals quietly cope with life with their own private programs of spiritual renewal and continuing education, right where they are in the familiar sights and tedious chores of ordinary life. Gleaning insights here and there from Scripture and learning from God's scientific practitioners, as well as popular journalists, they seek diligently to live life over again day by day.

They seek to avoid the bitter mistakes of yesterday, at least to a degree, if they cannot exchange them altogether for more constructive responses to life's challenges. Situations which they can neither alter, amend, nor reverse they hope to avoid, if not ameliorate with new courage, faith, hope, and love from God. From what other source can these spiritual powers come when other human helpers fail and one's own nature demurs or defaults?

There is only one way to live life over again now (aside from the scriptural promise of the resurrection), and that is to claim each new day as a portion of eternity, that dynamic now, which is fresh every hour and new every morning. This moment we live; this present minute we forge constructive links in our existence. And not all blows strike the anvil at the correct angle. The metal is not always red hot for shaping but must be plunged into the liquid fire of roaring coals and kept under forced draft in order to become malleable again to the smithy's design. Even then, after shaping it on the beaten anvil, it must be dropped into chilled water to be cooled and tempered. Can the fortune of a man's life over the years be less than the lot of a horseshoe shaped and fitted to a particular horse for a special function, such as a race horse or a dray horse? The psalmist sang many nights about the hard blows of God and existence, but he always looked for the morning with the assurance of God's new mercies.

I

How does one live his life over again each day with a fresh start? A bus driver ran away to Las Vegas from the boredom of his narrow route and life. The wheels of chance gave him no benevolence, not even a change, for he was soon back at the steering wheel, poorer and under severe disciplinary penalties.

The ancients knew something of the truth of each new day's existence which we must discover afresh in this generation characterized by permanent satellite stations, orbiting the ever-whirling earth.

> Look to this day!
> For it is life, the very life of life.
> In its brief course

29

> Lie all the verities and realities of your existence:
>> The bliss of growth;
>> The glory of action;
>> The splendor of beauty;
> For yesterday is but a dream,
> And tomorrow is only a vision;
> But today, well lived, makes every yesterday a dream of
>> happiness,
> And every tomorrow a vision of hope.
> *Look well, therefore to this day!* *

Unfortunately, some people stress life as a fixed destiny of incorrigible causes and effects. Others seek escape by denying any worthwhile meaning to life's struggle. A greater number acknowledge that life is as plastic as the potter's clay. The earth of a particular area may have its own qualities which become a given factor, but the moist, soiled hands of the potter can fashion and remold the lump.

Here one may say that the potter can rework it until it is baked hard, but then what? It is true that life has its limits. But even these accepted limits can be reused, reworked, and rearranged.

Perhaps the venerable cathedral at Chartres, some sixty miles southwest of Paris, may illustrate the principle. It is five or six hundred years old. During these centuries it has incorporated different styles of architecture from Romanesque to Gothic and beyond. Old foundations of one style support the towers of another type. The exquisite stained-glass windows of one century differ from those of another in color and texture. A destructive fire many, many years ago ruined the roof, which was replaced in different fashion. The ravages of two modern wars have swept by the cathedral. Still it stands, high-towering over the fertile plains and visible for miles

---

* "The Salutation to the Dawn," author unknown. Attributed to Kalidasa, translated from the Sanskrit.

away, a composite of many centuries, many storms, many craftsmen's contributions. Its many features blend into one cathedral, still motivating young and old to a new hope for life, for more beauty in existence, for greater love toward mankind, and for lasting hope beyond all tears.

Is not that cathedral of differing features something akin to what life is like for the ordinary mortal of no unusual distinction? He, too, builds new dreams on old foundations or even those of another person—his parents, his friends, or even strangers or foes. Storms and wars work their damage within and without, but still he keeps on building. In our own land everything seems to be required to be new. The old is often forsaken and removed. But in other lands, East and West, men have learned to incorporate the stones of the past into the present rebuilding. Whether it is a scarcity of raw materials or continuing sentiment that requires this, it adds to the building's beauty and interest. The same is true of a modern man or woman. The marks of joy and pain, sorrow and victory, mingle into a constantly new and continuously woven fabric that tells the story of a life deeply involved with God and man and the uncertain changes of the human struggle. A new life can be built out of old materials. The broken dreams, as well as broken stones, can be part of the foundation of an ongoing cathedral of life which may change its style because it incorporates new functions into its refocus of design and intention as the decades go by. One advantage of old cathedrals is that they provide a sense of continuity and renewal to life over centuries. Sometimes a more transient endeavor at church-building ceases to be useful and ends up merely as a garage repair shop, a warehouse for bulked paper, or a makeshift welfare office with plywood cubicles.

Building a life is like building a cathedral stage by stage. When Frances Willard was eighty-seven years old, she said if she could live her life over again she would praise more and blame less. Perhaps here is a clue from one of the earliest members of the women's revolution, indicating the possibilities of constructive change day by day. Another one said, "I would be more tolerant."

There are other clues on how to utilize each new day as one of personal growth and fresh development of useful attitudes. Concentrating on becoming a fully orbed person, one day at a time, is a worthy assignment. That means expressing the richness of God-created human life at the matured level one has achieved, whether it is twenty, forty, or seventy years. It means praising God in the skillful use of the physical body, the intellectual mind, the spirit and its emotions, all entwined into one inseparable entity. Like the American creed of one nation indivisible, so the human personality is one undivided unity of body, mind, and spirit. Each aspect influences the other as well as drawing meaning from the other part. Personality is not a train of separate cars—body, mind, spirit— which can be shunted and switched, parked and hauled away piecemeal. The various aspects of a person are a unity more like the whirling parts of a fluttering helicopter with its bird-like flight capacity. But when its counterrevolving blades cease functioning together, it is an ungainly and vulnerable bird. Just so is a person in his unity of parts.

At various periods of civilization each aspect of the body, mind, or soul has been glamorized or penalized in isolation, to the hurt of the whole person. The Christian view of life, on the opposite hand, exalts the unity of body, mind, and spirit as the special gift of God. To be truly human means to develop and use the body and the mind fully as well as the soul or religious faculty. It is not any tribute to God to disparage learning or to suppress the rightful use of bodily appetites and powers, any more than it is helpful to squeeze dry the emotions. Likewise, the opposite indulgence of whipping emotions into uncontrolled frenzy—either just for excitement or for ecclesiastical choreography (as King Saul did when the Spirit of God had left him)—is neither helpful nor characteristic of Christian renewal of life at its fullest.

To become more deeply human, one needs to exercise his body, mind, and spirit conjointly. Rest and exercise are as much a part of the devotional life as is the reading of the Scriptures and silent meditation. Charles Darwin, whose remains are buried in an honored place in Westminster Abbey, regretted in later life that he had neglected his spiritual culture for concentration solely on intellectual pursuits. A proper balance is the objective of living, not overcompensation of body, mind, or soul. A Christian should train his mind and every other aspect of his being as well, in order to enjoy God, glorify him, and serve him more usefully in this present world.

Walter A. Fox, an eminent creator of advertising, taught many young people that developing the personality on all its fronts was an arduous lifelong task. There was never enough time for it in long periods of repose, he indicated. Rather, one had to discipline himself to salvage meaningful fragments of hours in order to think, to read, to play, as well as to pray. Often the last light to go out at night was the brass lamp with the green shade where he sat reading a few lines more related to human existence than to the competitive edge of successful marketing.

One would probably not conduct his life much differently if he had a fresh grant of forty new years, unless he learned how to use creatively the constant stream of new life already coming to him in minutes, hours, and days, which are to be treated as rare jewels.

Newness of life comes in little things carried along on the stream of fleeting days. One high school boy saw it come to him in an impulse during the frantic hours of Christmas shopping. He was working part-time after school as a wrapper in

33

a variety store. Above the jingle and clatter he heard a pathetic young mother explaining to a tired clerk that she did not have enough money to accept all her layaway purchases for her children. She was thinking aloud of which one she could leave behind to balance the account she owed. In a moment the boy responded with his generous impulse. He whispered to the clerk, "Give her everything, and I will pay the difference." He might never have had quite such an opportunity for spontaneity and growth if he had lived two lives over. The possibilities of new life come of a sudden in the ordinary little circumstances of any day, not in the magical gifts of unexpected long years.

Sometimes it is possible to salvage life, but only with a great struggle, from the relentless crowding in of little demands and supposed obligations. The Bible describes this slow deterioration of one's span of years by saying that the little foxes eat away the vines and so the vineyard dies (Song of Sol. 2:15). In today's world especially, only the little things that abide with lasting value can help make each day new. Otherwise, we realize too late that hours and days have been lost even while they were new.

Time can be salvaged from wasted anger and irritation as well as from anxiety and revenge. What a noise there would be if everyone dropped and broke an empty glass jar each time one of these time-wasters consumed his moments. But then if the losses were dramatized thus, perhaps precious hours might be salvaged, and a life could start all over again instantly with creative love and productive work.

II

Generally, it is people who furnish us with the ways to live life over again. Even the stranger who enters our gate can illumine a new challenge, or silently reprove a secret fault, or genuinely engage us in seeing new life through his fresh eyes.

During a period of service in South India, an old man knocked on my door—just to talk, he said. At first it seemed like an interruption of study, such is our harried custom of scheduling every moment. Then it developed that he had walked five miles to engage in the adventure of this conversation. He was a wise man, and an engaging one, as well as informative and contributory to the process that ignites any conversation when two human beings seek to communicate with each other. The insight that flashed into view then has remained. Do we not often ignore the wealth of life available to us in the many persons who cross our daily paths? Without knowing it, we divert them with some sterile and customary greeting.

Even friends can assume in our minds the rigid and sharp outline of an old silhouette. There in black and white is our mental outline of friends and classmates. But we must remember that they have changed, as have we, during the slow weeks of familiar meetings and in the swift years of long absence or silence. Each one is a new and different person with joy and pain to tell about or share. "Old Joe" and "Dear Sara" are not the same as they were before. They have need of wisdom to hear, and they have love to share in return. But the loud good-nights, often heard in a jammed foyer of an apartment building, seldom provide a clue that once again life has moved too swiftly among friends who forget to notice its new offerings or recognize their own new needs. Yet each person could have ministered one to the other if all were more aware that life is lived over anew each day.

Have you ever heard anyone really respond to the banality, "What's new?" Yet each one could enrich the other if he shared his little new days with his friends in either listening or trusting. But so often we are afraid to venture. Then what we lose in our jocular words of conformity is worse than the high price we need to pay for individuality and creative living.

35

John Randolph of Virginia missed this truth somewhere in his eminent career. He was a noble person but not able to get near to people. He died sadly away from home in Philadelphia in 1833, when he forced his attorney to remain with him to the last flicker of the candle of life—lest he finish his years in solitude. If he had been less aloof, he could have had many friends to share his life and mourn his death.

The family is the place to learn how people can mutually enrich each other's lives. Here is a microcosm of learning, support, and interpretation which can enhance each new day. That is true unless the defense systems so characteristic of human strife prevent it. On the other hand, how strong are those who find their emerging personalities nurtured and encouraged by the support of parents and children.

Winston Churchill's father died January 24, 1895, when he was only forty-four years of age. Churchill wrote of his father's aloofness and then declared wistfully that in five more years his father would have needed him. Each person in a family needs the others—the word of encouragement as well as the ones of rebuke.

Thomas Carlyle failed in this same respect as well as in several undertakings before he achieved renown. He had wanted to be a minister, but that never seemed to be possible. He tried law, but that was no better. Nor did mathematics prove to be a rewarding field for his skills. Finally, he married Jane Welsh, and after that he found his outlet in literature. He labored diligently to produce his masterpiece, *The French Revolution*. Unfortunately, the maid of a friend accidentally tossed the manuscript into a fire and destroyed it. He then had to write it all over again. In this he was as persistent as he was creative.

But even such a genius of a man missed the new opportunities each day to enrich life in his family. He would often criticize his wife, Jane, and they quarreled often over the years. Yet he buried her with deep remorse. For years afterward, he would cry, "Oh! If I only had five more minutes with you." But clutching after more time is not as productive as using well the fleeting series of five minutes here and there which we have new throughout every day and night.)

Most people, if they could live their lives over again, would plan to give more love, to be more constructive and more understanding in their families. Today, even though the hour may be late, is a new day to begin right now.

> Oh, what a little time have we
> To gentle be, and kind,
> E'er we must mingle with the vagrant wind,
> The sleeping sea.

III

By now you can see there are myriads of opportunities for new and creative life every day all about you. Old patterns, fruitless endeavors, bitter mistakes are prodded into new redemptive situations by the mercy of God in the little unplanned events of ordinary days in the marketplace and on the highway.

The passing stranger who engages you may be an angel, to use an ancient figure of speech. He may even be unshaven, unkempt, or drunk, but still the flickering spark in him can kindle in you new compassion, new insight, new resolves, and fresh perspectives. In this he serves your need for inner renewal and the necessity for you to express yourself more and more as a fully developed human being, rather than to exist as a suppressed, defensive, or inhibited dignitary. Maybe, without the benefit of familiar cultural props, or with the addition of the same advantages to some needy vagabond, the two human beings alike could see each other more clearly under any street lamp. They would both see themselves as needful of God's grace and equally wasteful of his opportunities for living life to the full.

The family with its diversity of needs, interests, and temperaments is a ready-made environment for testing and development of new life. Robert Frost said, "Home is the place where, when you have to go there, they have to take you in." But can that not be true of other areas of God's worldwide family? Could it be fear in our hearts that makes us keep other people so far off? Is it possible that we could be newer and richer personalities as human beings if we accepted other races and other cultural groups more readily as being God's provision for variety and newness in our lives?

IV

There is, moreover, another area for discovering new life day by day. Paul declared, "What things were gain to me, those I counted loss for Christ. . . . I count all things but loss for the excellency of the knowledge of Christ Jesus my Lord: for whom I have suffered the loss of all things . . . that I may win Christ, and be found in him" (Phil. 3:7-9). Have we?

To dream of doing great things in some new faraway life is less worthy than trading off trivial preoccupations now in order to enjoy the treasures of a more worthy service to God and society today. Few persons do great things by direct and ambitious aims. Of course, some do plan and reach their targets, but even so, the world keeps moving beyond them.

What really counts is to use each new day to serve God and some great cause of his which lies beyond one's own years of accomplishment.

In Amsterdam, Holland, the Central Railway Station rests on thousands of concrete piers sunk into the marshland by the river Amstel. Hundreds of eager young American and German tourists seldom realize how the building rests secure and supports locomotives while they arrange their dream trips to Copenhagen, Vienna, and Paris. In a similar vein, few of us remember that we labor on foundations which other men and women have built. We in turn do but raise the scaffolding for others to add their creative services. No one lives his life by himself or for himself. He fulfills unfinished tasks of others to whom he is a debtor and prepares the platform or canvas for others who will finish the work. If men had built only the medieval cathedrals they knew they could finish in their own lifetime, there would be few Gothic structures left today. It is true that the new Coventry Cathedral has been built in one lifetime, but even that took almost twenty years of toil by hundreds of craftsmen and the converted energy of millions of people in the form of gifts of love and money.

Besides making an adequate financial living, a person needs to work for something larger than the tyranny of dollars, the whimsy of style, the capriciousness of opinion. He needs to labor for the abiding common good as in government, education, medicine, agriculture, and aesthetics.

The reason Paris is so beautiful today and the Jardins des Tuileries a refuge for hundreds of visitors is because a gardener long ago had a vision of transforming a dump by the Seine River and started a plan of trees and grass which others have completed since and still conserve. One man alone in his lifetime cannot hope to fulfill his dream or dream large enough if only his own years are to be the limit of his work.

The same principle is true of the church. The average congregation lives within the stricture of one single year's budget and one year's time span. But few hospitals or large projects of service and education ever emerge from such limited sights. It is only a large and long-range dream that challenges persons to make a vital church that can afford to harvest the present joy of invested hours committed to such a high goal, looming long beyond one's own years. Life seems adventuresome when each nightfall whispers that the day's toil has been for a cause larger than one's life.

That is what sustained Jesus in Gethsemane and on the cross. Without the long view, his sacrifice seems senseless. With the long view of God's caring, it became the secret of new life for all people who believe his words, that he who loses his life for the kingdom's sake will discover and find it more fully. And you can see that more is involved here than death.

If you would live for larger interests, if you would live your life over again, then see the possibilities near at hand. To embark now on a life of useful service having a significance beyond your own lifetime is already to have commenced living life over again.

The present period of revolution and disruption is not the end of the world, nor will it be the loss of all spiritual values. What is happening is that each gain of the past years is being tested. Some patterns will fall down but be rebuilt in part in the new forms to arise. More than ever in the twentieth century, this is a high day of opportunity to put one's energies into reconstruction and the discovery of new enterprises for mankind under God's direction.

We have had so many short-term renewals that we forget what a major upheaval really looks like.

The Renaissance, the Reformation, the Age of Enlightenment were all exciting as well as devastating periods of change. But dedicated men and women nurtured and guided them to good conclusions more often than we remember, sometimes even at the price of their lives. We, too, can throw our remaining new days into restoring the meaning of humanity, recognizing the dignity of all races, renewing the functions of cities as well as their aesthetic facades. There are a dozen other critical areas of service under God, because this is a period of enterprise in all situations. It is a time to exercise great faith in realizable projects here on earth. I have not singled out the church in this discussion each time because the church is a part of the whole fabric of life and no longer a thing by itself which can be passed by carelessly on the busy road of everyday living. The church will be revived spiritually when its disciplined members start living anew for God's ways in the human issues that are larger than their own lives and longer than their short years. This was something of the challenge thrown to Queen Esther by Mordecai when he declared, "Who knoweth whether thou art come to the kingdom for such a time as this?" (Esther 4:14.)

Uncover the Hidden Power Within You—
your capacity is ten times greater
than you know

You have deeper powers and capacities in you than you realize. Cogitation alone will not confirm this to you. Only the severe challenge of constantly changing circumstances will bring you to the point of discovery. The glorious prospect of each person around you, as well as yourself, is that in your present situation there are new powers and skills for you to use if you care to develop them.

Just to list your talents and skills, major and minor ones, would make an impressive catalog of abilities and powers. But beyond what you might tabulate, there are still other capacities in you not yet imagined.

The basic premise is that challenges, crises, work loads, and emergencies force us to unaccustomed levels of life. Not only do we have latent individual traits, but Jung's psychology suggests that some of the attributes of our forebears lurk in our being for further development. We are not isolated individuals. We are persons who stand in a transmission line of gains from human struggles over centuries which have left their influence.

We are not even alone in our calculated efforts for self-improvement. We respond to the demands and expectations of the community. Few persons make good masters of themselves. They need the outside stimulation of others in home or work, in school or church, to prod them to deeper levels of usefulness. Besides the prod of community expectation there is even an incentive to grow from an awareness of one's weaknesses, or, better, one's undeveloped aspirations can become a spur to renewed growth. Paul candidly acknowledged that when he was weak, then he became strong in the power of God (II Cor. 12:10). To know his limits drove him to greater utilization of divine wisdom and energy.

Most of us go through a turbulent phase at various points in life when we are unwilling to admit we can no longer do something as well as we used to do it, or as well as the new generation following us. But when we do accept that need or weakness, then we release ourselves to find other new skills or techniques. We also free our families or associates from the embarrassing conspiracy of adopting our self-blindness. It is a terrible adjustment for a person to give up driving his own automobile and to surrender to being a passenger for the rest of his life. But then how much more he enjoys the journey, and usually so do his companions.

No one has unlimited powers, nor has he utterly unfathomed depths to plumb for skills, talents, and attributes. Yet he has many more than he knows, waiting to be developed at certain stages of life. To gain them usually some lesser or outmoded practice has to be discarded. Here again the apostle Paul knew that dropping one phase was the price of gaining another and better one.

It is the abrasive shock of circumstances, the jerking pull

of challenges, the stinging judgment of other people which force us to discover new levels and new talents within us.

I

The reason we reach comfortable plateaus in life is that we tend to settle back at every newly acquired level until, prodded again, we spurt on only to repeat the same cycle. Whenever we reach a cruising level, we tend to stay there until stimulated to a new range. Toynbee simplified the formula for personal growth or social history as being one of challenge and response.

The unchallenged life or the unexamined one continues in the same direction until it meets a stronger force. Here is where private lives, schools, churches, businesses, and governments need challenges even if they do not need disruptions. It has been a long time since the Christian church has seen a coliseum with lions in it. Most coliseums today are skating rinks filled with the sound of waltz music. Maybe the stimulus to newer vitality in the churches will come in other forms than shaggy manes.

It does something positive to one's personal potential to live in the shadow of reminders of other people's courage and growth, unless one gets utterly desensitized to it. In many European cities there are chinks in the stonework of homes and public buildings where bullets and bomb fragments splattered to a pulverizing halt. In Paris stone memorials with flower holders keep alive the memory of brave persons who were felled on sidewalks and cobblestones for the liberation of that beautiful city in World War II. At Oxford near Balliol and Trinity Colleges, on Broad Street, there is a cross of cobblestones embedded flat in the middle of the street to remind all passersby that Bishop Latimer and Bishop Ridley were burned at the stake there in the sixteenth century for freedom of conscience and the reformation of the church.

There are other monuments besides markers of cruel deaths. Memory and books, music and art, stir the soul to redoubled efforts. Present crises and current major problems are more than annoyances to established living. They are raucous reminders that life changes, that there are deeper levels of life for young and old, that each age of a person has its own advantage to be used. These developments do not come automatically with each winter or the first check from Social Security in one's retirement. In fact, gains are not even automatic with every challenge; they must be seized and captured before they escape one's grasp.

Men and women have gotten along fairly well with well-organized systems that were founded on false premises or inadequate data. During the centuries when the earth was supposed to be flat, children were born, married, and died. Life went on as usual. But when the bold European navigators flung out their sails and courted the supposed abyss, they sailed around the spheroid world and opened up an entirely new era. We can hardly be expected to feel their emotion of elation these centuries later. But are we excused from showing equal bravery in breaking some of the myths that hold us still in bondage, knowing full well that they will be broken someday by our children's children?

When the earth was thought to be the center of the universe, artists painted religious pictures, and billowing incense made prayer times fragrant in the churches. But the earth was not really the center of the universe. Nor is the sun its center today, for there are other brighter suns than the one central to our earthly orbit. Life develops most when challenges are faced and comprehended to one's best ability, and when the major assumptions are kept under continual active examination.

It used to be a style never to retire. Then better economics and social customs nurtured a pattern of normal retirement for older persons. Now new ideas are fast developing as a result of military retirements after twenty years of service. People are retiring two and three times in the long span of forty years. Many are deliberately planning two or more professional careers. They go from the military life to law, or from professional athletics to insurance or banking, from teaching to the gospel ministry. A person need not plow corn all his life and then sit down to eat cornbread and molasses until he dies. He can learn to paint expressive art, write mellow tales, or weave lasting tapestries. Nursing used to be the domain of women. It is now open to men, just as some of their professions are opening up to women. A surgeon's widow became a rural minister of two churches. We just do not know our potentials because we have not thought in terms of the creative use of ourselves as we are throughout the years of our lives. Grandma Moses, with her bucolic paintings of red barns and pink orchards, is a symbol that each person has much more to do in life after sixty or seventy than he or she thought. It is only lassitude and custom that put a man on a golf course six days a week in retirement or make him wear out the wooden discs in endless games of shuffleboard.

II

So what does one do when he wants to discover new creative depths? Besides realizing the attractive possibility of it, he needs to do a little planning for such discovery over a span of years, whether he is thirty or fifty.

One cannot walk into a school, church, or a town hall and offer to be put to work doing "anything." Most people have to exert their own initiative to find the challenges, then develop their possibilities, and forcefully bring them to fulfillment.

An executive from a New York firm nearly went mad after his first month of retirement in Florida. He finally developed a career within his own past skills by helping his church as a part-time business administrator. That in turn put him in a position to help other men find places of employment. Soon he was running five different types of service, including job placement and part-time accounting assistance. A grandmother helped her married daughter go back to college in the mornings, while she herself finished up at the evening college sessions.

Not even the physical limitations that strike in the worst of times—in middle age or just before normal retirement—need shatter the dream of increased usefulness and the creative use of oneself as one is. It takes more than ordinary daring and determination, but when one's normal skills and powers decline, there are other ones, even nonmuscular ones, to be developed. One young paralyzed girl learned to draw with a pencil between her teeth. Another ran a telephone answering service. A hospitalized executive wrote a book of instructions. An aged lady prayed other people into lives of increasingly useful service. One woman, who warmed her chilled body with an old shawl, dispensed more grace and blessings with her generous smile and forbearance than many a professional person does with his anxiety hidden under a mantle of proper dignity.

Some people grow by taking on new assignments. It is believed that in a few years there will be more sensible volunteer roles of service available in the government or the church than just folding handbills for distribution. But each one will have to discover his own form of "Peace Corps" service and not wait for another to create it for him.

New assignments as well as new responsibilities and suddenly developing problems also stimulate growth. While change generally seems to disrupt, it may also create new levels of understanding and reveal new depths of skill or talent. The European city bomb craters of World War II uncovered long-hidden flower seeds of past years which germinated and bloomed even amid the rubble.

Our forefathers in the colonies declared a doctrine often neglected in modern politics; namely, that a legislative representative should return periodically to that place of residence from which he came. In essence this meant he should come back to live or work a while with his constituents, while someone else served in the halls of Congress. Thus renewed, he could be reelected for other terms after he had been that much closer to his own people's needs. I suppose this would be considered a threatening idea today for congressmen, teachers, and even clergymen, as I can very well understand it would be. But in the long run, it would make people more creative, stimulate growth, and possibly make life more enjoyable outside the usual rut—even if that rut is generously called by other terms such as longevity or seniority.

There is a new school for personal development that takes business leaders and professional men into the mountains or Everglades for survival training. They have also taken boys there from the city ghettos. The renewing principle is the same for both groups; namely, that confrontation with the bleakness and night noises of swamp, desert, or windy summit peak will stir the creative depths of a person to a new creative approach.

But what if you cannot afford the tuition of a training camp above the timberline? Then you can find a useful substitute training right where you are. The people and places around you are different. They, too, have changed since last you categorically gave each a mental value and ascribed a hairy face mask for each one marked either "I like" or "I dislike." Some people and situations are better, some worse, but both can challenge you to deeper growth. You are different too. Therefore, you may draw them out to a finer degree of response than once you did with a caustic quip or lifeless eyes, coldly watching while you correctly stated some formal greeting.

People used to walk past the quaint brick row houses on East 11th Street in New York City and admire their black iron railings with pleasant vines reaching up toward the Manhattan skies. They had no inkling that impatient young people might be making bombs inside one book-lined library or fusing explosives down in the basement dining room. But a sudden burst of flame and thick billowing blackness changed the whole block in a moment. Gone now is that entire row house. Scorched are the walls on either side of the cavity. Fresh cement and new paint around new glass panes, still bearing the maker's seal, identify the repairs to neighboring houses. Passersby walk more slowly now and stare. How things have changed! And they really have for you and me, too, in an explosive sort of way, demanding our creative response.

III

Encouraging others is one good way to alter your own life in response to the present explosive challenges. If you start to help people, their needs draw out your own responses. To lead others successfully usually means that one will also try out new ways too. That is what most fathers do with the graduation presents of bicycles they have purchased for their daughters or the mechanical toys they have hidden for their sons until the Christmas season. Our interest usually follows our involvement as much as the reverse of that proposition is also true. In fact, it is more so. Involvement leads to interest. Action leads to further action and opening possibilities.

A census taker who found a family in critical need went to the city welfare agency merely to secure immediate help for the family he had met in passing on his numbering rounds. But it led him on to a larger involvement in social rehabilitation for others and later into an entirely new career of social service. It is not useful to wait for people to encourage you into new and growing situations. Rather, it is better to encourage people at your hand—the policeman, the newsman, the store clerk, even your own employer. There is no one who couldn't use a little encouragement. For in giving it we make ourselves as well as the other person more creative.

IV

There is still another way to be creative and grow. That way forms the elemental basis of old vaudeville comedy acts. Someone suddenly throws a teacup to a clown who is holding a pile of dinner plates in his arms. Surprised, the clown reaches for the flying cup, but down drop all the plates to splinter on the floor.

The Bible puts this truth more eloquently when it admonishes us to lay aside the weight that hinders us and the sin that does so easily burden our paths (Heb. 12:1). The idea is that some things have to be given up to do other important things. We cannot do everything, even though we wish we might, and we try to squeeze them all in. Just today, for example, there were two profitable discussion groups to attend on the status of modern churches in England. There were also scheduled outings to go punting on the river Thames and a cricket match to watch, besides two good books to read, not to mention watching the Edinburgh games on television. I almost had to strap myself to the chair. The other things all had to be passed by in order to finish this chapter.

It is not always a matter of clear choice or obvious selection where one has to let go. There are outmoded ways of doing things or expressing life; there are outworn ways of achieving that have to be discarded too. Young people have their privileges to grow and so does maturity. Later years can be as rich and adventuresome as are the reckless ones of adolescence—

even more so, for one knows generally who he is and who he is not. But choices still have to be made.

V

Preoccupation and predispositions need to be laid aside for newer levels of loving, caring, and growing. Jaded interests need to be stimulated by adding new interests, not by jazzing up the old ones. A man may pass from a consuming interest in stamp collecting to a new level where he touches it only lightly, as he develops the collection of his grandson. In the same way interest in one's church probably waxes and wanes —just as does that of any healthy parson—but neither need run away to escape the ennui. There are much deeper levels of worship and service than the average member or clergyman ever dreams—so much so that their discovery might cause one to run with rejoicing to tell the Savior what he already knows: that life is much more rewarding than the average person permits it to be.

One angry young man accosted his preacher with the peremptory demand to have his name taken off the membership list, because the church no longer meant anything to him. The patient minister acknowledged the request in the affirmative but asked first for a favor. Would the young man mind going for one hour on that Sunday afternoon to read to a young blind college girl? He answered, "Of course not," with some bravado and considered the deed an inexpensive way to soothe the broken relationship with the church. But later, when he returned with a new vision of meaning and life service in his eyes, the old minister only grinned and nodded when the youth murmured, "Forget what I said about dropping my membership. I have a new job to do now."

VI

Another way to grow creatively is to utilize the present situation and one's talents to their fullest degree. Today's pattern for organizational thinking is along the lines of systems analysis and subsystems. For example, three lines of fabrication converge at the point where a whole automobile emerges. One system fashions the bare chassis and frame, another line builds the engine assembly, and a third one welds the body unit which is lowered on top of the engine and frame. Within each of the subsystems are small parts, often manufactured outside at specialty plants; for example, door handles, engine spark plugs, and automobile radios. But they are all brought together to one finished, total system of many parts.

What this means is that any job in a subsystem takes on a luster and usefulness in the light of the whole system. Miss Sullivan played a subsystem role of support to Helen Keller, who became a world symbol of courage. In a midwestern hospital one man ran the overcrowded parking lot so well that it ceased to be a source of irritation, and he became an inspiration to the physicians and visitors who reflected his friendly and courteous management of a critical parking problem. Most assignments and jobs have a higher potential for creative development than we can see in them without continuing reappraisal and continual refocusing.

Just to see tomorrow's task with more imagination could be the beginning of a more creative life. Even that will later yield still more creative revisions. Look at how the old victrola has been restructured for stereophonic music. One had thought the radio had superseded it, and radio men feared television had put them in the shade. But recreative and imaginative evaluations have redeemed both instruments to unique and useful functions.

Since most of us have succumbed to secular interpretations of business life, we forget that basically all labor and service is for the work of God's kingdom. But when a new emphasis is placed on a job in its relationship to the kingdom of God, it yields more satisfaction, less fatigue, and much more enjoyment because of the higher perspective. A man can dig a ditch listlessly, but if he learns he is rescuing a worker from a cave-in, the shovel will swing faster. When a job is reviewed in its service to God, it makes more sense, or more sense dictates changing that job into one that does serve the Creator's lasting purposes.

Pascal once said, "Always keep your eyes open for little tasks, because it is the little tasks that are important to Christ." The limits of your life only form the channel of power of your usefulness. Right where you are now is the place to uncover the hidden power of God within you through the creative use of yourself as you are. Abraham Lincoln said as he emerged from the great depression of his painful responsibilities, "I cannot succeed without God or fail with him." Life was intended to be much more than a grueling endurance race. It was meant to be a growing experience that is creative to oneself, of assistance to others, and productive to the kingdom of God on earth all the days of one's life.

II. The New Never Comes Until We Let Go the Old

First Steps to Forgiveness— a way to overcome the barricades

Forgiveness needs to open the door to further creativity in a person. Life does not come in neat, tidy packages. It does not even balance up at the end of every month or year. There are some irretrievable losses and a few permanent scars. They have to be reckoned with in the spirit of forgiveness, like the Lord's attitude on his cross, or else the creative forces within you stagnate into bitter gall.

Creativity involves the risk of error and even failure. To be unwilling to take the risks of life is equally as destructive as to undergo them. It is just not so obvious. There are two aspects to the main creative energy of life under God, as we know it. One is the donative or contributive side of life. The other is the retributive or punitive aspect. The one is positive and the other is negative. Too many people go on punishing themselves and other people, rather than running the risk of accepting liberating forgiveness in Christ and resuming their creative or contributive life functions.

One can become so obsessed with his weakness, failure,

blunder, sin, or incompetency that he uses it for an excuse to resist change while he goes through the familiar futile tasks and comforting habits that appease inner fear. But such contrivances of compensation never really work for long.

Jesus taught a more courageous way of dealing with some situations. He said that shaking the dust from one's feet and passing around the focus of trouble (once it has been acknowledged and dealt with) was more useful. He taught the necessity of forgiving others seventy times seven in one day. Not to forgive or not to accept forgiveness is to become one's own prisoner. Man finds his deepest renewal in repentance and the subsequent freedom to re-create. His inner release from guilt or anxiety permits him to express himself freely, to experiment with life, and to trust the open relationship with God for approval of his innovations. One can come back quickly from failure in the experimental attempt at better living without worrying about offending God or running the risk of his abandonment.

One of America's great theologians put his finger on it this way: "The ability to judge friend or foe with some degree of objectivity is, in the ultimate instance, a moral and not an intellectual achievement, since it requires the mitigation of fears and prejudices, envies and hatreds, which represent defects, not of mind but of the total personality." *

This is similar to the Scripture's injunction, "If I regard iniquity in my heart, the Lord will not hear me" (Ps. 66:18). This is no call to puritanical perfection, but it is an instruction to seek identity of feeling with God by securing forgiveness for one's blunders and by granting the same grace to those who have trespassed against us. There is enough residual anxiety within each one, and such a confounding awareness of his ability to do both good and evil, that almost everyone has both a general and a specific need for forgiveness in order

* Reinhold Niebuhr, *Faith and History*, p. 12.

to release the creative aspects of ordinary family living, daily productive labor, or far-reaching social involvement.

In Christopher Fry's play *A Yard of Sun* the father of one character vanishes suddenly one night because someone has betrayed him to the occupying troops. Yet no one in the Italian village or his family knows who the betrayer is, and each suspects the others and also himself for some careless thing he may have said or done. In the end it is his own daughter who in anguish discovered to her regret she had told her trusted friend where her father was hidden. It was she who let the secret slip. But all along the other members of the family were afraid of themselves, too, much as the way each of the twelve disciples asked the Lord who should betray him—"Lord, is it I?"

A creative life is based on a predisposition or fundamental attitude of forgiving others out of sheer gratitude that one has himself been richly forgiven by God. There is plenty to be forgiven in every life. There are chafing limits to one's own personality, skill, and ability which have to be reconciled, or else one goes through life with secret wounds. There can be human annoyances in the best of families, calling for a daily unction of forgiveness and forbearance. Other people, too, have quirks to be tolerated or endured, but they are quirks only to the beholder who must in turn forgive them and himself for his sensitivity. The best of human nature is still something of a burden to the inner person as it deals with paradoxes, ambiguities, as well as temptations of the flesh or, worse yet, of spiritual pride and malice.

Unfortunately, some people follow the painful path of punctilious legal rectitude as a way to God. They never fail to cross every *t* and dot every *i*, but they miss the human spark, warmth, and inspiration of loving and serving God joyfully. They have no forgiveness, nor can they give forgiveness. But if they could lay aside the secret weights within them, their lives would become richer in understanding and deeper in loving-kindness.

There is an old story of how to catch a monkey in the jungle without injuring it. A fresh coconut shell is opened at the top about the size of a half-dollar. A knotted string is run through a small pierced hole at the other end of the shell. The trap is laid some yards away from a person hidden in the bush where he holds the string. When the monkey grasps the fresh coconut meat, he won't let go, and so his own clenched paw traps his hand inside the coconut, which is quickly hauled in by the cord, and the animal is caught. Without forgiveness and the freedom to abandon the past, man, too, gets trapped in his own excessive grasping and holding.

I

Forgiveness releases barriers between people and within each one. Life's communication between people, at its best, is an interpreted exchange of feelings through a latticework of misunderstanding of words, tones, intentions, as well as meanings. The practice of liberal forgiveness is a practical necessity just to converse in ordinary exchanges. It is much more required where there is a rigid generation gap, a racial sensitivity, or the age-old complex difference of a man and a woman. The communication utopia we seek is not a land where each one clearly hears or understands the other. It is a state where each proffers generous forgiveness to the other person's halting or explicit words, and lets him emerge beyond the shackles of his verbs. If we ourselves have doubts, fears, and ambiguities, we shall need an equal amount of forgiveness, too, because we do not always know our own minds, any more than does another person or a group.

The Bible states quite simply that one should leave his gift for God at the altar and run home to be reconciled before he gives it to the Creator. The same is true in domestic life. In a mysterious sense a boy has to forgive his father in order to hear him—forgive him for his powers and weaknesses, his humanity and his authority. Likewise, the father has to forgive his son for clumsiness, ambition, foolhardiness, and maybe even lack of respect during certain years of his development. The secret is to forgive first and often, in order to listen carefully before one speaks his own rushing words and thereby needs himself to be forgiven in turn.

Forgiveness dissolves hurts and dissipates anger. It dampens the reverberating overtones of revenge which stir the strings of the heart with their old injuries and fantasies of conquest or retaliation. Forgiveness puts a limit and a lid on insult, slight, and injury.

II

Forgiveness precedes and generates repentance, rather than follows it as a condition of restoration. The usual affirmation is to declare one will certainly forgive another person (or race or class) if they will only show proper remorse or regret. This becomes the condition which then is used as a lever of manipulation, or the contingency which provides an excuse for withholding forgiveness. The biblical idea of forgiveness, however, is to grant forgiveness freely in order to generate repentance. Repentance becomes a fruit of forgiveness rather than a cause of it. Scripture avows, "While we were yet sinners, Christ died for us" (Rom. 5:8). It is not that we loved him first, but that he loved us first, and freely gave himself as a ransom for our sins before we turned to him in gratitude.

A soldier in Fort Dix had been punished many times for a series of minor but irritating infractions. He would not adjust to the military system. All the punishments normally available had been used by the court to deter and to influence him toward right conduct. Nothing seemed to work until a young trial officer petitioned the court-martial to grant forgiveness to the boy and provide an opportunity for him to straighten himself out. A senior officer replied, "Nothing else we have tried has worked. Let's give this suggestion a try." The soldier did respond to this new understanding and strengthened his own self-determined cooperation.

This truth applies in many personal situations. In the popular film *The Sound of Music,* the leading lady wins over the stormy and arrogant family of the baron during their first meal by her own forgiving acceptance of them—before they had accepted her—as they do later with great affection.

Professional jealousies, family quarrels, international tensions, as well as domestic and commercial strife, can be lessened and settled sooner by the generous use of wholehearted forgiveness. It is the very energy of personal rehabilitation and character change. "We love him, because he first loved us" (I John 4:19).

III

It is even more important to recognize that forgiveness fulfills the capacity of a person and helps him to emerge in fuller development. More people emerge under forgiveness than are coerced into change by threats or revenge.

Senator Walter George was one older statesman whom President Franklin Delano Roosevelt sought to purge. The senator accepted the face-to-face challenge to his seniority and tenure in office and stumped throughout his state politically as he had not done for a long time. He was reelected by his aroused and loyal constituents. But never once after victory did he vote in the Senate in a way to vent any retaliation or revenge on his President.

Someone will say that forgiveness is too good a method to be true. Yet it worked in Illinois politics just as it worked in the case mentioned above from the Southland. There in Lincoln's territory the principal leader of the party used to consult with his critic and even use his honest services on committees. As a result, former Senator Paul H. Douglas served his state better because by forgiveness he was able to utilize the brainpower of one he could have hated, ignored, or blocked.

IV

This principle is equally true in training young people and in helping the black race, or any other race or minority group, to find their destiny. We have tried to forge the strict mold of our children. We try still to lay down the terms for black cultural emergence. Neither way will work without sufficient forgiveness to enable young people, black or white, to rise freely from experiments and some failures to find out for themselves their own new world and its relation to the whole of life. Sometimes we even have to forgive people in our hearts because they seem to have brought in a better world than our old one, and we are shaken and envious of it.

John Wesley, the founder of Methodism, was an able English clergyman before he ignited the fires of social renewal and religious inspiration. But he was a formal, cold, and revengeful clergyman in the beginning years. Even his expedition to Georgia to convert the Indians turned out to be a failure. Inwardly he was afraid, while outwardly he served God. But all that changed on May 24, 1738, at 8:45 P.M. in London, when he attended a small meeting of devout Christians. His heart was warmed. Once he felt deeply forgiven and loved, he became the unforgettable spiritual power he was and an indefatigable leader of Christ for the people of many generations.

V

The practice of the spirit of forgiveness makes it possible for people to be agents of reconciliation among others. This

61

can be performed for one's own family or for strangers met in the course of life.

Dr. Martin Niemöller of Germany described his prison experience under Hitler's regime. One thing he never forgot happened as he was being led down a long dark tunnel. His heart was heavy and fearful. The guard marching behind him gave no indicative muscle movement of sympathy, or hatred, or identification of any feelings. But as he marched stoically behind Martin Niemöller, he spoke into the darkness for the comfort of his prisoner, "Thou hast been a shelter for me, and a strong tower from the enemy" (Ps. 61:3). That experience and phrase kept Niemöller alive in spirit for another span of months.

The same type of spiritual renewal came to a small group of minister friends of the late Daniel Poling. They had grown apart through neglect and differences over the years. One Lenten season in Syracuse while he was preaching on forgiveness, Poling felt a compulsion to telegraph words of forgiveness and reunion to his friends, located in New York and California, as soon as the service was over. Quick replies returned the proffered affection. Forgiveness, with its own powerful initiative, had reunited old friends and become an agent of reconciliation.

Church congregations were meant to be unusual fellowships of forgiveness for both individuals and social situations. The New Testament says to restore a sinner more often than it says to cast him out—in order to purify the group or punish him. The greater renewal of persons takes place in the spirit of acceptance, in forgiveness, and in restoration. A man should be able to go to church to find forgiveness and to practice forgiving others. More likely it is that he will be judged and started on the futile path of striving for prestige and comparing for self-evaluation. However, judgmentalism changes fewer people at the deeper level than does the overwhelming sense of having been freely forgiven by "love so amazing, so divine."

The strange reciprocity of the religious life is the experience that he who has been forgiven must forgive others. The reverse is also true, that you cannot give others release in forgiveness until you yourself have received the lavish forgiveness of Christ. If God for Christ's sake forgave us, then we for Christ's sake can forgive others and so release the creative energies and talents in both.

When a person has been forgiven, he sees new vistas in life, new potentialities in other people, new designs in his own life. Some of the dull frustration and the sense of thwarting of existence is removed. Criticism can be evaluated instead of scorned and rejected. Drudgery becomes something of a challenge and a new task. The sense of forgiveness accomplishes these things. The echo effect of past sins and mistakes of older years ceases to mar the present acoustics of listening to God's new words of hope and peace. Before forgiveness brought its cleansing and liberation, life was more like listening to music recorded on some audio tape full of hisses and scratches of unerased background noises.

For most people the most important liberating gift of their years, or in their power to bestow on others, is a fresh experience of God's forgiveness to set them free again in the creative role he intended for them to fulfill. Forgiveness by Christ erases the past so one can write afresh as he seeks to refocus his life in however many years lie ahead.

How to Love People You Don't Like—
they hold the key to your happiness

Every person needs other people to become a fully developed personality. But the interaction with other people in the home, at work, and in society at large presents one of life's complicated problems. A person needs to interact with others for his own development as well as that of others.

One of the myths prevailing in the folklore of how to live in the modern world is the idea that one cannot love a person if he does not like him.

A careful reading of Paul in I Corinthians 13 will indicate the general Christian belief that love is action on behalf of another person without regard to limit, condition, or illusion. This is a realistic way to get along with people we may not like. No one ever really knows enough about another person at any given moment or stage of development to say truly and finally that he does not like him.

Usually over the years one learns that God in his wisdom has made people of great variety and vast differences. The very presence of these divergencies can serve a useful end in any situation. Getting along with different types of people is a way to find a broader support for one's own personal development and enrichment. No one can be all things in his own life. He learns to depend on the complementarity of others who have skills that he may lack and of rendering aid to those who may need what he possesses.

The Scriptures, as well as common sense, teach that it would be a tragedy if the human face were all nose or all ear. All people have talents of one sort or another. Not everyone should try to outdistance his neighbor in every respect. If there were not two people on either side of the net, then how could a game of tennis proceed?

Getting along with a variety of people, including those whom one may not like, at first is a spur and a stimulus to one's own personal development. Usually we do not like people because of some flaw in ourselves which we find reflected in them, or the suggestion of such a flaw, which makes us uneasy without even being aware of the reason. To learn how to put up with the flaws and even the blunders of other people, without the excuse that we don't like them and therefore can't love them, is a stimulus to personal growth and maturity.

There is another reason why learning to get along with people of such different temperaments is a means of enriching oneself and at the same time of enriching the other person. Getting along with other people strengthens both the individual and the other because one seeks to interact and usually to put the best possible interpretation upon the other person's actions. By doing this he helps the other person emerge into what he truly wants to be.

In sketching with pencil on paper one doesn't erase every line but continues to stroke the pencil boldly until the image is clear, and then erases what is not needed. So one develops his personality by attempts, failures, and repetitions until he perfects the graciousness of the kind of living he wants to contribute to society. In helping other people to develop and in recognizing their need for development, we unconsciously develop ourselves.

One of our most challenging ministries is to learn how to love people we may not like. On a cruise ship out of New York a young honeymoon couple came late to their assigned breakfast table. As they approached the table for four and saw the other two occupants, they were startled. The bride's hand instinctively drew back on her husband's arm, but they sat down. A very attractive young woman greeted them cordially, but they returned her warm greeting with restraint. What fixed their eyes and troubled them was the gray-haired man beside her. His face was contorted and scarred, apparently from flames or some serious accident. He could not smile and he spoke with difficulty. When something seemed to be humorous, his tongue hung out.

Afterward, the girl said to her young husband, "I cannot sit there anymore. It will spoil the whole trip." So they managed to avoid eating at the table until the next day. Then while taking a promenade on the boat deck, the other girl from the table joined them and said, "Do you mind if I speak candidly with you? The gentleman with me is my father. Of course he appears ugly to strangers, but if you knew him as I do, you would agree that those are beautiful scars. You see, we were camping in a tent in Colorado when the fuel oil in the stove caught fire. He saved my mother's life and mine. Mother has died since. The scars my father bears kept me whole and healthy. Now do they seem any less disturbing to you?"

That night the honeymooners went back to their table at the proper time. Somehow the face which was so immobile did not seem so distractive. Later in the evening they all danced together. As the young bride said goodnight to the girl's father, she kissed him and whispered, "You are beautiful."

67

None of us knows enough about anybody else to say that we do not like him or that we do not love him. This is our essential service to one another every day, especially when we remember the man on the cross on Good Friday. He does not expect us to love everyone by the law of compulsion. Nobody can be compelled to like everybody. No one can be constrained really to love anyone. It is a futile proposition of religion to say that we should go out and feel love for everyone, even for Jesus' sake, for we will only do it when we want to do it. We cannot do it by argumentation or compulsion. But we can look at life, especially in the big cities, as the world's laboratory for proving our religion which is rooted and grounded in a divine love to us and consequently reflected to others.

In the Bible the field of human relations is set apart as the grand experimentation for a person to know if there is a God, or if he loves that God. The Bible says that any man can say he loves God, whom he does not see, but the vital experience in religion comes when he loves the man he sees but doesn't like. There is something in learning to love another human being that helps a person to love the God whom he cannot see.

I

Love that comes from God through human beings has tremendous power to help and to heal. We know this because our popular magazines describe its effectiveness so frequently in a secular context. We are so used to the topic that we forget that love is still dynamic and that most of us only half love God, and hardly love our neighbors, and may not even be comfortable with ourselves. Despite this, most of us prattle about love wholeheartedly. The point to consider now is to embark upon a vast adventure in daily life amid uncertain circumstances, testing one's ability to love people who are not easy to like.

In Johns Hopkins University, experiments have been made in this field from several viewpoints. A most attractive one was in the Pavlov laboratory. They discovered in the experiment of giving an electric shock to a dog that if a human being stood there and patted the animal, it practically neutralized the negative shock effect. Even if a human being were just present in the room when the shock was applied, the negative reaction was still mitigated. They went even further to discover the ripple effect of love reflected from one human being to another while he suffered shock in this same fashion. Turning the experiment completely around, they found out that one could suffer in his heart a shock effect which was more destructive than the electrical one if someone created unpleasantness by stimulating a painful past memory.

We can apply this truth in our daily work. We can bring encouragement to other people just by being near them. In our calloused conversations, where we are often crude and critical, we stir people with a negative shock greater than the painful muscular distortion of an electrical impulse. Yet we also have the same power to help in a positive way. We can best practice this by making an effort to select someone in every situation to whom we shall give our utmost spiritual support, in order to strengthen them in their own secret battle to become a fully developed person. We need to make it our business to help make people happier day by day in their own struggles and to help them in their efforts to emerge as their best selves.

Not only in the Pavlov laboratory at Johns Hopkins but also in their sociological department they have made another marvelous discovery. One professor had sent his students out to interview 200 boys in one of the depressed sections of the city. From their observations they had prognosticated that 90 percent of the boys would be behind prison bars before they were very old. Then some fifteen years later, another team was sent out to follow up on the lives of these 200 boys. They were able to find 180 of them and interviewed them. Only four of the original group had gone to the penitentiary. The interviewers asked each one how he had made out in life and what factors had chiefly influenced him for good. Slowly the answer pattern began to appear. All of them referred to a certain teacher by name. When interviewed, the old retired teacher was asked what her technique was that she had used so effectively. She simply said, "I just loved those boys."

The Scriptures declare. "Love suffereth long, and is kind; . . . believeth all things, hopeth all things" (I Cor. 13:4, 7). Love does not think evil, expectantly hoping it will happen. Love changes the world. Love never fails. We all subscribe to this proposition on Sundays, but we have yet to experiment with it on weekdays. It is so easy for all of us to write off the obligations of the healing mystery of love by saying that we do not like certain people, so how can we possibly love them!

But the power of love can be seen dramatically when it works in its opposite direction—the power of anger or hate. In one Chicago hospital they had a little boy who was cured recently. He was nine years of age and his name was Joey. Before Joey would eat his evening meal, he drew invisible wires around himself. Then he took his milk straws and fashioned them together in a long tube which he inserted through the imaginery wires. He did nothing that was not mechanical in its design or approach. There was nothing wrong with him biologically except that he lived in a mechanical environment. The only way to reach him was to pretend that you, too, were in the game by lifting the imaginary wires in order to come near him and give him some more milk. When he went to bed, it was the same thing. He shut himself off from the world mechanically.

From what kind of a home did this boy come? He came from the family of a talented, dedicated naval flier who, in giving service to his country, was seldom able to be home and play with his son. The boy's mother was an attractive, educated woman who did not want to be bothered with the arduous task of bringing up a son. She turned him over to others as much as she could. The poor boy was neglected, so he built his own mechanical world to save his heart from the ache of the loss of love. This was judged later when at the hospital they picked him up, loved him, put him in the tub for a bath, dried him, and put him to bed regularly with tenderness. He said to the nurse, boyishly, "They even kiss you when they put you to bed here." Then finally one springtime, he wanted to make a poster for the parade float. He put on it: "Feelings are more important than anything under the sun."

There are people who are dying for a little bit of love. "But how can I love them if I do not like them? If I show love to strangers, I might get myself in trouble." How then can we show love in action creatively without getting sentimentally involved? This is fundamental because some people are so hungry for the power of love in their lives that sometimes they will commit crimes just to get attention and care. Gabriel Marcel, the distinguished French thinker, wrote that love is the key to personal development and the betterment of the individual in society.

We can see to what great lengths people will go to find this creative and healing love in any issue of the evening newspaper. A few months ago on a Friday evening, Angelo Zayas, thirty-one years of age and an unemployed factory worker, is reported to have called up a friend who happened to be a postal inspector. He cried into the telephone, "My friend, I have just been released from Lewisburg Federal Penitentiary as a narcotics patient, but I am back on heroin again because of the pressure of my friends. I can't stand it

71

outside any longer. I have just robbed a mailbox, and I want to give myself up to the authorities."

The inspector friend suggested that they meet at his office and go together to the marshal. Mr. Zayas was arrested, indicted, and sent back to Lewisburg. His last words to the judge were, "Thank you. Now I am the prisoner of love and care again."

The shattering question is: Does a man have to stage a mock robbery in order to have the loving protection of a federal prison? Might it not be possible in the world's greatest republic for men and women who can so freely give Christian love to bestow it on a narcotics victim like this man so that he does not have to ask for aid in reverse? We are so quick to excuse ourselves from this loving redemptive ministry because we often behave like Thomas Carlyle did to his wife, Jane Welsh.

They were once entertaining a very prominent visitor, and he was making sure that the visitor knew of his importance. In one of the pauses or gulps for air Carlyle heard Jane breathing heavily, and he said sharply to her, "Jane, I wish you would not breathe so noisily." A few years later when she did stop breathing altogether, he read her private diary, and only then, insensitive man that he was, did he learn what grief he had caused her with his sharpness all their married life. In his grief he cried for another chance, but there had hardly been any five minutes in which he had not criticized her.

We are God's angels on the earth, the only embodiment of the gospel there is in secular society. We often are so quick to criticize, so loath to redeem people, so fearful to attempt to love those whom at first we do not like. It is possible that in our communities this week some person will commit a crime in order to be protected from the lovelessness of a city or community where, like the boy with the talented parents, he will line up invisible wires to protect his own heart from coldness and hurt.

Jesus said, "A new commandment I give unto you, that ye love one another" (John 13:34). Love suffers long and is kind. Love never fails. The last thing to give up is love. Faith, hope, and love—these three never fail.

II

Have you ever thought of some of the reasons why we do not like people? We are all educated twentieth-century people. We know something that people did not know in 1875. Today we know that we automatically flee in childish fear from people who are different, from people who speak differently, from people who dress differently, from people who smell differently, and from people who sing differently. Children look at a Greek soldier with his fluffy skirt or stare at a Scottish kilt because they notice quickly anything that is different. We look askance at anyone who threatens our ego patterns with difference or with change.

We also do not like people who project their hostilities on us. The last man to get out of a taxicab slams the door as much as if to say, "That's for you." To the next person who gets in, the cabdriver may say gruffly, "Where do you want to go?"

Inwardly we think in reaction, "I don't like this driver." Then we look at his name on the license card, and we think to ourselves that the peculiar name proves his surliness. "Just look at the way his name is spelled," we think. "They are all alike. It just goes to show you."

When we arrive, we say to those we meet, "Guess what? I got one of those so-and-so taxicab drivers today." And so we go on spreading prejudice and antagonism.

Actually, what really happened was that the driver was angry at the last fare, who probably was upset with someone else, and so we are critical of his name without reason. Whether that name be Swedish, Rumanian, or of New England ancestry, it makes no difference.

Also, we do not like people who invade our territory, those who crowd us in the subway, or even those who take our favorite pew in church. It is the same thing. It is an invasion of the territorial instinct in every being. A man says, "I don't want anyone cleaning my pipes when I put them in the rack. If they are dirty, let them stay dirty. Don't touch them."

And a woman says, "I don't like anyone in my kitchen upsetting the silverware." This is our instinctive reaction. We do not like anyone who changes anything.

We do not like people who reflect our weaknesses. If we have a habit of being late, how critical we are of other people who are late. If we are scatterbrained, how impatient we are with excited and forgetful people.

We have a common phrase, "It takes one to know one." We do not like people because we see in them some of the things we do not like about ourselves, so we say, "How can I love anyone I do not like?"

The Bible goes on to say that all areas of life are responsive to our giving this love even where there is strife. When we see two people quarreling, there is an opportunity for love to try to neutralize it. Wherever you see anyone debasing or humiliating another person in any way, wherever you see immoderation, wherever there is the spirit of revenge, pride, selfishness, and insensitivity shown in legal rigidity, or in extreme cold formality, these are the areas of division, distortion, and cruelty, where you can let love shine through in your kindness.

III

How can we get this power of love from our Lord Jesus Christ to work in this kind of an environment in the twentieth

74

century? One of the first things we can do is to define it. Love is generosity in action. You do not have to like people just to be generous to them. Love is constructive action in another's behalf. Another man put it this way: "It is commitment without any guarantees."

Emil Fuszner saw in his evening paper the picture of a man, standing beside the inert body of his dead wife after an automobile wreck. We all know people who have had accidents far away from home. But Fuszner wrote to the man every day for four weeks and also sent flowers to him. This was his way of being a practical Christian. Two months later the daughter of the man wrote, "You kept my father alive when he lost all hope at the death of my mother."

What did Mr. Fuszner get out of it? Just the joy of being God's servant. He made a habit of this. He read again in the paper that someone who had been in prison in Illinois for a long time had never had a single visitor, so he went to see him. The man was in on a conviction of murder. He claimed to his visitor that it was all in self-defense. It developed that he had been up for parole repeatedly over a period of twenty-two years, but since no one knew him well and no one appeared to be his sponsor, he could not be released. This modern Good Samaritan decided to sponsor Richard, and today the older man is living a redeemed and productive life.

About fifteen years ago Fuszner saw a newspaper account of a Civil War veteran, one of the last few, who was living in a shanty. He went to see him and asked him why he lived under these conditions and had no pension. The man replied, "I do not get any pension because I deserted when I was fourteen. However, I reenlisted and was pardoned, but I have lost my honorable discharge papers." Mr. Fuszner spent months finding the records. He got the man a pension and saw that he was placed in more suitable housing. Again what did he get out of it? Just the joy of being God's messenger.

You do not have to like the people to perform deeds of love. You can keep yourself filled with the love and marvel of God and reflect it to others. As much as you are filled with the love of God, you will be able to give it out to other people. The arrows, slings, and darts that prick and wound us daily will bounce off more easily. Learn to love people in general because there is an infinite variety of human beings. Set people free in their spirits.

Often we are tyrants and try to possess other people as well as control them, rather than letting the fullness of their personalities emerge. Parents often say to their children, "How can you do that to your father and mother?"

But what right do we have to be tyrants over others, and particularly the lives of our children? God gave us our children to love. Let them be free and they will love us for it.

In his wonderful article on how to get along with people, C. S. Lewis pointed out that God knows two things while we know only one. We know how bad other people are. God knows that too, but he also knows we are just the same as other people. There is enough truth in this to keep us humble before God. The thing that we hate in other people is usually what bothers us. "Why," we muse, "it never dawned on me, but I do the same thing." It is rather humiliating to discover this. But if God can forgive us, then we can forgive other people. The Bible says that if we do not forgive others, God will not forgive us.

Let people be free. As an old mother used to say, "Let them be," not "Let them alone." Let them be because the love of God that fills us also projects on them.

We can do good deeds in God's name for his love's sake. We can attempt to neutralize strife. There is not any wrong situation which cannot be ameliorated by our tenacious love. We can try to make people happier where they are so that they can become their better selves. We do not have to be obvious about it, nor do we have to ask for a written receipt for the kindness we show them. It is possible just to be a silent messenger of God's love and let his Spirit bless other people.

The Bible says, "Love never fails." The suggestion, in the Greek language of I Corinthians 13, is that love is never hissed off the stage. This is our secret fear, that perhaps we shall be considered fools if we show love in the modern world. But the truth of the Scripture is that love never fails.

On January 13, 1954, Maurice Ewing was serving as an oceanographer of Columbia University on a 200-foot schooner called *Vema*, some 200 miles north of Bermuda. During a fierce storm he was swept overboard along with others, some of whom were lost. He was finally rescued and later wrote this letter, in essence, to his children:

Dear Bill, Jerry, Hopie, Petie, and especially Maggie—all five of you:

Yesterday your Daddy was swept into the raging January Atlantic. I nearly drowned. For hours I thrashed about and tried to cling to life. The only thing that kept me going was the knowledge of the love of you children. After awhile, Bill, Jerry, Hopie, and Petie, it was only the voice of little three-year-old Maggie's love which kept coming to me to urge me on until finally I was rescued. Never underestimate the power of your love.

Your Daddy

This is what Jesus is saying to us. As we go about the streets of the city, we need to remember the Man whose scars were for us and whose name is Jesus. The world looks at his cross and remembers that even he cried out, "My God, why have you forsaken me?" But if you will step up a little closer to that cross, you will hear him also saying, "Father, forgive them. They do not know what they are doing." By our forgiving people for their ordinary humanity and loving them by active service on their behalf, we release them into fulfillment of themselves, and in doing so we deepen our own lives in refocus as well.

Finding God's Plan in Your Work—
puts you in tune with cosmic harmony

The separation of religion and daily work is almost over because the swing has gone too far. The same is true for the myth that corporate business has little obligation or concern for the social conditions of men or cities. These dying viewpoints of the last half-century served as a sort of adolescent rebellion against the older truth, that men and women find themselves more deeply when they seek God's plan in their daily work.

God seems to have come more clearly to persons on their jobs than to people sitting in churches, as far as the biblical stories go. Subsequent and sophisticated histories of people of faith point strongly in the same direction of refocus. Peter and John, the disciples, were washing their nets, a tedious task like cleaning old varnish brushes. Ananias was making ceramics when God sent him to heal Saul of Tarsus, the converted rebel.

Joseph, the patriarch, became the food administrator of

Egypt, and Nehemiah served as the Persian emperor's wine steward and cupbearer. In this latter function God used him to effect the rebuilding of the walls of Jerusalem after they had lain in disrepair for almost a century following the holy city's fall.

Even Jesus was a carpenter more years than he was an itinerant teacher of righteousness. His divine ministry was directed to tax men, merchants, vineyard owners, soldiers, fishermen, and investment bankers more than to professional religious leaders. His most noted convert, Paul, was a tent-maker, a producer of canvas and fabrics. It is no wonder that Paul was able to challenge and win the faith of Lydia, the businesswoman of Philippi, for she was a dyer and seller of rich purple textiles.

Most people spend the larger part of their creative hours at organized work and commercial enterprising. They carry home to their children their moods and attitudes which they reflect in their home life. Even after a man's retirement from work, his life-style reflects his years of employment in a particular trade or profession. Where a person works is a major place to practice refocusing his life, because there he comes in contact with the major forces that influence him economically, politically, and socially.

The working situation for most people has been a rapidly changing one in a swiftly shifting age of technology. Even some young men have been phased out of special tasks by new techniques, new substances, new forms of merchandising. Since this process will continue to affect most people, one needs to perceive God's plans in daily work which can produce inner satisfactions to be fulfilled in many different jobs, rather than to stake all one's rewards and career on one skill or situation. When work and commerce are seen as the tools of God, they can be redeemed as vehicles of service to mankind and as sources of necessary personal satisfaction. Of course, one objects that assemblyline methods can destroy a man's spirit and rob him of purpose and significance. This is one of the major challenges of refocusing one's job, whether one builds automobile engines, controls the speeding ingots of steel through the rolling mills, or tediously fits electronic components that may decide the life or death of an astronaut 238,000 miles out on the moon. Satisfaction is still mainly a matter of the attitude one brings to work as much as the reward one hopes to take away from work. Any job can have its higher or lower scale of motivation.

Everyone was jolted into an emergency status when several babies died in an eastern hospital nursery because of a bad formula mix. The moral side of every job came to the front when it was discovered that salt had been placed accidentally in the sugar cannister in the formula kitchen. The same sort of moral earnestness was awakened when a series of automobile brake failures caused a manufacturer to recall 85,000 cars for repairs. Even the most menial and mechanical jobs hold a life and death coefficient in this highly industrialized and technological society.

An attorney like Ralph Nader may be a gadfly to manufacturers and a tedium to newspaper readers, but he has dramatized a truth that God does his moral business in commercial offices, financial houses, manufacturing plants, and in consumers' heartaches, rather than just in the holy rooms of church buildings.

I

Daily work would be enhanced if it were seen again as the normal activity of doing God's service, hearing God's guidance, fulfilling the Creator's plan. Churchgoing, too, would become exciting again, as a way to report back what God had done through the week's work. Worship could become exhilarating as a renewal of insight to keep on serving and as a developer of new areas and fresh ways to minister in daily toil.

The quality of human service in business depends on whether one sees it also as God's work. Unless toil is done for the glory of God, it becomes very difficult to sustain it for the good of others. It is even less likely to be motivated just by the hunger for money, strong as that is. Beyond a certain basic need for money, the tedium and burden of service are just not worth it—unless one keeps his primary vision, that he is doing God's work and serving God in other people's needs.

It is a fruitless age-old debate whether one cleans up people first to clean up city streets or whether the reverse is true. Probably both are true at once, or neither is a sufficient explanation of the present crisis. However, a clean city does encourage the endless task of renewing beauty in any tired worker. A workman can press on further when he serves a loftier goal than just a clean street or a cleared desk. Something of a vision of God's lasting goals for mankind has to be seen beckoning beyond the chores of daily existence.

The Bible teaches that most of the men God works through are men at their tasks—wine stewards, artists, dancers, musicians, herdsmen, ambassadors at court, owners of private and corporate businesses. All of this is God's work just as much as that of a prophet or a pastor.

On August 16, 1962, Amos Alonzo Stagg, the great football coach, was one hundred years of age. Friends held a centennial birthday party for him. He told them how initially he had felt he should become a preacher, but the University of Chicago had called him into athletics, where he became a leading figure. He said, "I realize that God called me not to preach in a church but to preach on the scrimmage line, and I have had a great ministry coaching football these many years."

82

Rudyard Kipling wrote a poem called "Mulholland's Contract." Basically, it is the story of Mulholland's coming across the ocean on a boat where he attended a shipment of cattle. As the ship went through a storm, some of the partitioning broke down, and the cattle started squeezing and horning each other. Mulholland, filled with a sense of his duty in this crisis, climbed over the stockade among the cattle and tried to separate them to maintain order and to keep them from panicking. In the midst of that danger, with sweating bodies heaving against him and horns plunging toward his ribs, he said, "O God, if I ever get out, I will give myself to your service. Spare my life and save me."

They reached their safe harbor. Kipling had this moving answer at the end of the poem: "God said, 'Go back to the cattle.'"

Men and women in their daily tasks and skills are doing God's business more than anyone in the so-called professional religious world. It is more important to be a good bank president, a good cashier, a good secretary, a good stenographer, a good elevator operator for the glory of God than it is to be a preacher on a Sunday morning.

This is the religious concept of life, that a man should see his daily toil as God's toil—building the city, cleaning the streets, preparing the food, generating the commerce which sustains the life of the people. The Christian concept of work is that God calls every person in his total existence to the vocation of being God's servant.

It is not just the nine-to-five job that is God's holy calling. It is the total life. Even when one is at leisure, he is still part of the main calling to be God's workman. Each one has his stages of education, his leisure, his so-called years of economic livelihood, and then his retirement years. But all of these are part of one continuous sweep of service for God.

Work is part of God's productive plan as well as his spiritual program. Work is man's spiritual expression of his total being. Work is where he lets his creative impulses out by using wood, money, or plastics, or taking a group of people and creating harmony out of their diverse skills in order to make life worthwhile and to enrich existence.

II

One person still counts in this enterprise in a pluralistic and mechanical age. It is a subtle temptation to imagine that an individual so longer counts at all in an increasingly technological society, managed by persons with all sorts of ideals and religious values. Unfortunately, this temptation to personal diminishment has accelerated a standard of the least common spiritual denominator, just as mass manufacturing has standardized interchangeable parts.

But this condition is not a new personal problem. Keeping in line, failing to rock the boat, minding one's own business have always been part of man's spiritual struggle in simpler ages. Nehemiah was beset by these personal attacks on his motivation when he rebuilt the wall of Jerusalem in 444 B.C. He was able to persevere against odds because he kept saying to his detractors, "I am doing a great work, so that I cannot come down; why should the work cease, whilst I leave it, and come down to you?" (Neh. 6:3.)

It is not a sufficient excuse to succumb to pluralism of values and mechanism of procedures, and say hopelessly that one can no longer do God's work in the world of daily toil. Nehemiah fought off political pressures, threats of congressional investigation, economic sanctions, and libel to his character. Joseph, the patriarch, even went to jail for his personal integrity when he was falsely accused of disloyalty. Even in prison he was able to serve God and his king, ultimately procuring his vindication and release to larger usefulness.

The value of the least common denominator in modern life

is a constantly shrinking one, unless a few people peg their standards of integrity as a model for all. The respected Society of Friends did this during a corrupt period of English history. Some equivalent practice must be found in America's present period of moral lassitude and easygoing corruption, by whatever felicitous terms it is called. An article in a respected news journal called the rash of thefts of stock certificates a "shortage in the box." The report of annual losses by theft in an Ivy League university's bookstore, amounting to $200,000, was considered part of the cost of modern life by another commentator.

Appalling as these crimes are, they are neither a new condition nor the whole story of this generation's efforts to refocus itself in daily toil. The pressures of coercion, the threats of reprisals, and the fears of individuality were significant in every cultural phase of earlier years in biblical history, just as they are today. Men and women refocused their lives then in the worst of times as they did also in the wildest profligacies of the court of King Louis XIV, and as they are doing now in the daily power struggles of executive suites and foremen's locker rooms. The odds are no easier or any harder. The issues are always a challenge: to do God's work in one's daily toil, to maintain one's own integrity in a pluralistic society and in a machine culture.

III

One reason for the mythical separation of work into sacred and profane callings was an attempt to escape the ethical tensions presented in daily work. It was easier to say that business was business and God's work was religious. Today the biblical viewpoint is returning to eminence by reason of the burden of corruption in a high style of life and because of the boredom of noncreative money-making, as paradoxical as that may seem to many.

The biblical viewpoint of life has always seen work and service as a trusteeship of God's money, materials, and objectives. With such an ideal, a skilled manager can rise to great responsibility without corruption of his pride or pocketbook, because all his power and privilege are exercised under the discipline of God. He keeps himself from corruption and from being broken as a clay idol of success. He enjoys his service to God and man.

By the same token, the person who cleans the tables in the company cafeteria or sweeps the concrete floors of the factory assembly line knows that he, too, is an important trustee in the whole project. The kitchen worker keeps men healthy, and the factory sweeper prevents disastrous injuries or ravaging fires which in one night could knock out jobs for hundreds of families. Thus dignity is sustained inside the blue-collar man as well as in the white-collar person, and there is a mutual respect for each other's contribution to the enterprise.

A sense of trusteeship would provide an incentive to the present concern for a restored ecology of urban and rural environment. Only the alarm of necessity has convinced modern man that "the earth is the Lord's, and the fulness thereof" for man to hold in trusteeship (Ps. 24). The spacecrafts' cameras and instruments have convinced people that there is not unlimited clean air and pure water. The earth-system's supply has to be recycled and nurtured responsibly. Otherwise, foolhardy indulgence of natural resources is as culpable a practice as robbing a child's piggy bank to buy one's cigarettes.

The beauties of Paris by night, the galleries of London by day, the architecture of Vienna, and the plazas of New York could not be preserved without a sense of trusteeship of the common good. When one generation lives only for itself, it impoverishes its own years as well as the future. When it builds and replenishes for others, it rewards itself. The same is true of persons and of institutions.

The same false myth that pretended to divide the sacred and the secular maintained a corollary dividing the material from the spiritual. Actually, Christianity is a materialistic religion. Before one agrees too readily and construes that phrase as a calumny, let it be clear that God has always used a policy of incarnation to reveal himself. He came to mankind in the person of Jesus of Nazareth. He uses the materials of his earth to benefit his people. He deals in actuality and not just in idealism.

A Christian identifies his motivation and his utilization of substance as a spiritual obligation. His job, his home, his factory or office, his automobile, and his golf clubs or boat are all held in trusteeship for some higher purpose. This does not take away from his enjoyment. It increases his joy and diminishes his anxiety. He uses what he has as a trust to be returned in as good condition as he received it, not dissipated or buried as did the one-talent man with his treasure.

IV

The major refocusing of life will probably be in terms of economics and daily work. These are central to personality. An Ohio policeman was renewed in spirit by a radical conversion of attitude and practices. His partner in the patrol car noticed it within the week, without being told about it. He inquired, "What's come over you? You are more relaxed and not so jumpy and angry. You used to curse everyone."

One can see such a rich outlook on one's job in the uniformed guard at the Panthéon in Paris. His authenticity is more than a uniform of authority. His eyes and voice reveal an admiration for the heroes of France, who repose in the echoing chambers of that citadel of national remembrance. The guard makes their memories come alive for the weary traveler. He transforms a pedestrian task of guarding a shrine into a sacrament of reviving hopes and dreams of service to one's own time of trouble. But the same sense of high calling is often repeated by secretaries and receptionists in hundreds of offices. They do not do any different work than others; they do the same work differently as a sacrament to God.

On my first day in Amsterdam I boarded the trolley car to go to the Central Dam. No one had warned me to buy a ticket first or else to enter the front door of the trolley car and pay cash. Everyone else boarded at the rear door, so I joined them. A sign in English, however, warned that there was a fine of $25 for riding without a ticket. Threading my way through the double car, I explained to the conductor-motorman my ignorance and need of a ticket. He stopped at the next traffic island in that busy city and helped me purchase the required ticket from the machine mounted on the signal post. He could have glared at me, ignored me, upbraided or arrested me. Instead, he created an everlasting impression of a motorman who guided a trolley for something more than modest wages. He was victor and not victim of his machine.

There is no perfect job for satisfactions. There is only a continual refocusing of the person's attitude, which when brought to his job transforms the most creative or the more menial tasks into opportunities for rich service to God and men.

Robbie is the first name of the rosy-cheeked Australian gentleman who keeps the porter's lodge at Mansfield College, Oxford. Peering out of his window by the entrance quadrangle, he serves as friend and benefactor to students and masters alike. It is a pleasant thing to return to the college after hours spent away and signal one's return to Robbie or to receive a message at his hand. By any measure his duties are demanding, multitudinous, and tedious, but his spirit makes them a ministry of grace to his students.

Some professional men and some elevator operators have the same high conception of their function. Others serve only as the minimum requires in order to secure a paycheck, and thus they deprive themselves of all other rewards and stimulation in their jobs—and such satisfactions are present in every task.

Eric Hoffer, the eloquent longshoreman in San Francisco, wrote, "It is futile to judge a kind deed by its motives. Kindness can become its own motive. We are made kind by being kind."

V

In a secular and mechanistic age, where people seem almost as disposable as paper products, a man can attempt to refocus his life at work simply by affirming life again in all his human relationships. This will be a religious exercise as well as a social one. To help people, to ratify their skills, to encourage their efforts, is to double one's own usefulness.

Eric Hoffer has said that there is in human affairs a reciprocity and an equilibrium of cause and effect. The cause can be as much affected by the effect as the effect is produced by the cause. Indeed, it is often possible to produce the cause by staging the effect. Whatever good or evil is started in life tends to justify and perpetuate itself.

It is still possible to maintain the human equation in this urbanized technological era. It takes more courage and innovative skill to do it, however, but the opportunity is present in every job and occupation. The potentiality for serving God in daily work is not lost in metropolitan situations; just the expectancy of it diminishes under the pall of anonymity.

One way to overcome this psychological pressure of conformity at work and the limitations of strict job classifications is to try giving oneself away as well as just working for pay. The usual cry is, "I am not paid to do that." Such may be the case. But there is still the possibility and challenge of giving oneself and one's service away beyond requirements. The common creed is that one will work harder for more pay, but the usual practice is for one to advance when he gives more of himself to the enterprise. One teacher advised his students to work at the achievement level of the next higher pay rating above them. They gave themselves in work at the next higher level and soon reached it. Even if a man did not achieve his dream, he would at least relieve his boredom and resentment by the spirit of his attitude of creativity and generosity. This too would have its constructive side effects upon his work and his colleagues.

The exhilaration of a refocused life can be experienced most directly in the area of one's daily toil. There, life can be performed as the sacrament of work offered to God, and there can be discovered the rewards of service to mankind in his name. "Inasmuch as ye have done it unto one of the least of these my brethren, ye have done it unto me" (Matt. 25:40).

III. There Is More Than
One Way to Banbury Cross

Listen to God's Voice Within You—
*   he can turn you on when you are off*

Up to this point we have talked about refocusing life because circumstances and people are in constantly changing conditions. This merits a periodic fresh look at life and a midterm correction of its course toward your renewed goals.

By making frequent checks on your life's focus—certainly major ones every decade—you can live your life in a new direction from this point forward. You may be limited in some aspects but you are never trapped. There is always a new life in the forward direction with a fresh constructive attitude.

Even the one- or two-talent man can use his life productively and creatively as it is. There is more and more mobility in life careers as well as the established frequency with which people move to other parts of the country. Moving one's furniture is not the only way to get a fresh start, however. It can often be done right on the spot where failure or disappointment has taken place.

Forgiveness of oneself and others has to have its healing way in order for the new life to prosper. Cherishing resentment is like pouring gasoline on a fire. The one who pours gets hurt. Even the best of persons needs to accept God's forgiveness for conscious faults done against his own accepted high standards. Then, too, there are others to be forgiven for clumsy or even malicious acts. Forgiveness is the key to the gateway of a new life.

There is another key, too. Listening in a deeper way to God and life will free one from the shackles of group conformity and the enormous pressure upon everyone to conform to the general mean which is established in a community.

We all hear more fresh stimuli and signals than we can act upon. We all conform to what other people average out to say or to be thinking. As a result we all average well, but we gradually succumb to other people's expectancies for us rather than achieving self-direction along a conscientious road.

Most of us would be shocked to learn how much we miss in a day when we could have heard more, or more clearly. In our zeal to speak we do not listen deeply and carefully, so our conversations pass each other or overlap.

There is a wide spectrum of signals to confirm or rebuke one's daily course in life, just as in the rainbow there are invisible hues of violet and red, fading beyond human sight at either end of the spectrum. These stimuli come from God, nature, man, and one's own conscience, as well as deep consciousness of the past. Changing circumstances need to be evaluated correctly. Other people's judgments, together with the accumulated voice of the church and history, all help to clarify what one can discover of the purpose of God for his life.

The conscience is not infallible, but it does inform us of any gap existing between one's own high estimate of the best and a contemplated inferior step. The Bible, together with church history, is like a rich set of tapes in a computer bank from which one can check out various possible answers and their results.

In the field of listening to God for guidance about a change in one's life course, common sense still plays an honorable and spiritual role. God is unique, but he is not a fool. He deals with modern man faithfully and reasonably as well as by increasing degrees of insight. The essential need in refocusing life is to ascertain God's general direction as well as one's own normal and responsible preferences—which need not be considered contradictory to the divine will. Furthermore, to enhance a new focus in life, one needs to enlarge his range of listening to life's signals as found in people, history, Scripture, as well as conscience, insight, and surmise. "In all thy ways acknowledge him, and he shall direct thy paths" (Prov. 3:6).

Leland G. Griffin said that the will of God is always, for every life, that life's most perfect unfolding. The will of God is love in action on our behalf. He takes nothing away which in itself does not take away from us. But we need the courage to believe and act on this by listening. There is always a higher channel to listen to in the heart's secret meditations, where life is settled. There is always a lower frequency in the spirit to attend beyond the common chatter of life where opinions and half-truths pass undetected as normal static to intensive listening to God.

Loys Masson, a French novelist, suggests in his book *Advocate of the Isle* that there are signals only the foolish ignore. There are levels of being where no man is an atheist. This phenomenon of unbelief is strictly confined to people who do not know their own depth. But these signals do not come easily, nor are they recognized without probing, checking, making mistakes, and trying again. Even the apostle Paul was on one journey he thought to be of God when he was deflected in a different direction by further spiritual stimulation in a dream. He envisioned a man in Macedonia crying, "Come over and help us." Paul went and it was proved out by his going.

Thomas Powers said that one of the glorious and terrible facts of life is that God's will is in exquisite reciprocal relationship with the will of man. Ralph Waldo Emerson added, "The crises of life are not births, marriages, deaths, or great occasions, but rather they are quiet afternoons at the turn of a road when new thoughts and impulses rise in the mind."

Two of the most famous cases of inner listening to God mentioned in the Bible happened to people who did not even know the Lord. One was the young adolescent Samuel, who was told of the end of Eli's destiny, and the other was Cyrus, the Persian king who was instructed to help return the Jews to Jerusalem.

People receive nudges from God's Spirit in many natural phenomena besides dreams and hunches. He uses the elements of nature to stir the mind. A wild storm on the mountain or deliverance of a ship from the raging sea may stir resolution and clarify instructions for a person.

Besides the normal reflexes of the body revealing the inner thoughts, the sensations of the body can also induce deeper moral reflection. In the book of Esther, the king had insomnia and summoned a courtier to read the royal annals to him. It was there that he learned of his failure to bless Mordecai, who had once saved his life. In rewarding Mordecai from that moment on, he saved all the Jewish people from their persecutors. Paul saw his thorn in the flesh as a means of deeper spiritual focus in his life.

One way to see the Bible as an aid to deeper listening to life is to consider it as a vast computer storing programs of input by inspiration. It tells of how God led and man reacted over a period of two thousand years. A familiarity with Scrip-

ture can give one many case histories in which to see con-
nections with today's issues, and from which one can derive
precedents or principles for adjusting to the present.

All of one's sense of spiritual guidance should be checked
with Scripture to keep one's judgment sound and to prevent
the uneasiness which comes with an extreme sensitivity.

There is still more input to the computer-like testing of
one's judgment. There have been two thousand years of church
history beyond the Old Testament. The struggles of sincere
men and women in that span can offer counsel now when
consulted. As a result, one can have the vicarious experiences
of men and women in the Old and New Testaments and in
the early and late periods of church history to evaluate and
check his own growing focus on life and sort out his new
insights for corrective soundness.

This value will appear more useful when one remembers
that all signals and stimuli need to be interpreted. Printing
appears as letters arranged into words which have to be de-
ciphered before the meaning of the sentence can be comprehended. Musical vibrations likewise have to be translated.
Usually one needs to hear a piece of music played all the
way through once in order to comprehend it better on the
second time around. Blips on a ship's radarscope need to be
interpreted, even as does an oil painting or a piece of sculpture. This is an interpreted universe in every respect.

The presence about us of signals in ordinary phenomena
and the necessity for interpreting them into action is not only
true of listening to God but of listening to man as well. Listening to people is arduous, not just because we all desire
eagerly to tell our own experiences, but because there are
many wavelengths in any conversation. There are the sound
waves of what was said, what was meant, and what was heard
or understood. In addition, each person speaks or listens on
the levels of self-awareness, his unconscious life's depth, and

his present responsive alertness to others. Besides these levels there are also the different media of communication used in symbols, facts, and preparatory attitudes.

It is much harder to listen than to hear. One must know the speaker, his life, and his general line of thought. We all tend to speak in shorthand symbols, which the familiar community knows but which the outsider does not comprehend. These have to be explained to him in the common life. Listening needs to be practiced at home regularly and its greater extension certainly would enhance the life of trade and international politics. No one can see the rest of the world as strangers when once he has refocused his life on Christ, who is the Savior of all men who believe. He will then see others of variant races and cultures as friends whom God made, rather than as threats to his own security.

Perhaps the greatest adventure that comes from more intensive listening, besides a richer sense of seeking God's direction for life, will be in observing what listening does to other people. They emerge as they are listened to. The depth of their existence comes out when they are heeded rather than cut off curtly in the flat dimensions of black-and-white literalism. When people are thoroughly listened to, they hear themselves think in depth, perhaps for the first time. They detect the rich overtones of integrity within themselves and catch the buzzing sounds of false reasons or tarnished values. People grow up in proportion as they are listened to intensively.

By the same token the listener grows too. Holding in check his inadequate judgments and imperfect responses, he economizes on turmoil and irritation. If he pauses long enough, he discovers new information and more useful solutions to human problems.

Listening to God and fellow creatures is more than mere politeness. It can be turbulent listening, even defiance or rebellion. Job, the sufferer, argued with God in his pain to ascertain the reason for it all and to work out a way of handling the endless nights of agony. He was not condemned by God for his debate with the Almighty. Most earthly parents grow, too, to a point where they learn to deal with the anger of their children. They may even discover quirks or attitudes in themselves which enrage their offspring such as those which caused Paul to write, "Fathers, provoke not your children to wrath" (Eph. 6:4). But most of us exasperate others unwittingly, until we learn with our children to see each other constantly in a changing focus of growth by intensive listening —and it must be a two-way conversation. A candid exchange is better over the years than passive resistance that politely alienates forever. It may be that the Lord himself enjoyed the prodigal son more than the hostile good brother.

So we develop, too, when we listen, as well as when we are listened to. How hollow our grievances and complaints sound when prayed aloud. How murderous are the echoes of our wrathful pledges of vengeance when we say them aloud also. Our assurances of faith, by the same token, sound stronger when affirmed aloud to others or even to oneself in the secret silence of a bedchamber or hospital room. "The Lord is the strength of my life; of whom shall I be afraid?" (Ps. 27:1.) Try it yourself right now, while you read.

At this point someone might raise the question, "What do I listen for—from God or man? What can I expect to hear?"

Probably you will hear nothing external to yourself. Certainly Paul's companions on the way to Damascus did not hear the voice of God as he did when he was converted. But you will probably hear insights in your heart—sometimes wordless convictions strengthening the rightness of a resolve made rationally with arithmetic or pencil and paper, weighing lists of pros and cons.

You may also hear substantial overtones to ordinary conversations and the performance of the tedious chores of life. One hospital surveyed all its discharged patients for their evaluations in order to render better service. When asked what she thought contributed most to her recuperation, other than the professional staff, one lady made this reply: "The cheerful demeanor of the mop lady dusting my room became my daily expectation in my loneliness." The radiant lady with the mop became God's messenger (but she had no wings, of course). The forgiving understanding of a state policeman's warning may speak more of God's forgiveness to you than a printed text—especially when you know in secret you have been driving under pressure.

God's dealing with us and other people is not always a religious matter. It is a matter of life. Religion was made to serve life, not life to serve religion. It is not always a religious circumstance when God deals with us. Few meals would be enjoyable if they were endless rounds of admonition, "Eat that—it will be good for you." Dining becomes a sacrament because love and fellowship mingle with the unconcerned enjoyment of God's bounty which brings nourishment to us without anxiety. In the same way God speaks to our listening in natural events.

Some listening will be a more thorough reading of Scripture —perhaps "savoring" would be a more fitting word to use in connection with a refocused life. Many of us have used the Bible as a yellow-paged, classified telephone directory to find help in time of trouble. It was more usefully written as a revelation or as God's love letters to be read, absorbed, and reflected all through the years.

Other forms of listening (for one type of listening increases the skill in other ways) will include silent waiting, as the Quakers do in their attendance upon the Inner Light. Most people will feel slightly ill at ease after ten minutes of this until they practice handling it. Then they will be surprised at their calmness and the discovery of direction or deliverance in living. Did the Lord take a pocket transistor radio with him when he sought solitude in the desert? The reason was more than that they were not yet invented. The issue is that we all need to be still and know God at a refocused level, fitting our maturity and adulthood in the modern century.

Few contemporary Protestants know how to listen with their fellow congregational members. In fact, for many the idea is a foreign one and offensive. Surprisingly though, it is a fundamental idea in the New Testament. The Holy Spirit guides the members of a congregation as an entire family unit when they consult as a whole, with one another, and pray together. Since this is a neglected practice in a day of highly individualized, private religious practices, most believers do not know the joy of joining with others to pray for direction of life. The steps of progress in the New Testament were confirmed at the gatherings of the apostles and the believers. Disciples did not just go off on their own intuitions. They checked up on their beliefs with the others.

Modern congregations could help their young and old members by more group life. Young people would be heard and would share in the counsel. Older members would be remembered and would feel their recognition when life had begun to fade for them. The mind of Christ would be more clearly seen by prayer, conversation, and mutually helpful participation. Do you see how different this is from adopting a resolution by an executive committee for issuance to the press, in today's ecclesiastical practice? The pressure of changed lives instructed by one another can be greater than the proclamation of a printed position. That may be the reason why young people sit down and block the road sometimes. It may be an ill-advised action for them to take, but at least it is personal, real, and gets a reaction one way or the other. Where their process of activism fails is that they are not invited back into their congregations to give an account of their happenings and the reasons for them. It might be fruitful for open discussion and mutual discourse to evaluate some actions of protest which often seem more like public display for the mass media.

If persons and families, as well as congregations, would listen together to each other and to God, they would find clarification of their convictions and courses of action. That is what the early disciples did when they had to adjust as Jewish Christians to the dramatic influx of Gentile converts. Some of the strong Judaistic Christians wanted to make the Christianized pagans perform the Jewish rites also. The controversy was bitter and prompted Paul's Epistle to the Galatians as well as references in his other letters. The radical solution of accepting Gentile believers without making them perform Jewish rites was decided in conference together and with prayer.

Listening does more than confirm directions and create harmonious decisions and compromises. It also prompts motivations to share, to do, to go, to act in response to community and world needs. This is true for both individuals and congregations. Impulses checked with the judgment of other believers can provide new thrusts of larger service or innovate entirely new patterns of usefulness to God on this earth. A refocused life of an individual will reciprocate with a refocused life of a congregation containing such persons. Inventive change is needed in the spiritual life just as much as it has come automatically in the technological world.

If the present generation keeps on adding years to the average longevity, people should plan and listen more carefully on what to do with their longer lives. The blessing of added years and the promise of human organic transplants bid one to plan a refocused use for his whole life as well as the added span, long or short. Since life is already longer, perhaps one should plan carefully to earn his support and daily bread in two or three different cycles or careers and then devote a fourth cycle in retirement to public service or to creative arts or handcraft. These ideas now sound far-fetched because they cannot be executed as career plans without longer preparation. But the years will come when longevity will be used more creatively because we shall listen earlier for guidance to choose and to change work habits and pleasure patterns.

At the present time retirement plans are often a patchwork or a guess when they should be the integral part of a useful life of working and listening. Perhaps the same indictment is true of even the good progress made in ecumenical understanding of Christian bodies around the world. Both personal life plans and ecumenical reformation need to be even more radical and inclusive. They need to be a refocusing of the whole as an integral unit, rather than a mere addition to a mainly independent structure of a life or of a church. Listening might encourage one to build his life for the retirement years of service, or listening might encourage denominations to shed their superstructures entirely for a newer and more simplified instrument of the divine Spirit in the modern world.

As in a vast air terminal one can concentrate on the noise and bustle of weary and anxious travelers, or he can listen deeper beyond the noise level to a solitude of reflection. So one can take his refocused and newly creative life back into the immediacy of a noisy market, or he can listen there to the deeper yearnings of man and the promptings of God. Whatever the confusion may be of the moment, there are signals all about to be perceived and verified that will lead on to fulfillment of the hope of our lives.

We rob ourselves of joy and achievement by reacting to the nervous insistence of passing impulses, the corporate pressure of the herd instinct, and the restless void of purposelessness about us. The decision now to develop the discipline of listening to God will sort out the finer impulses to growth, the warmer values of social relationship to people, and the continuing purpose of God for each one's many phases of developing life.

"Speak, Lord, for thy servant heareth" (I Sam. 3:9).

Personal Endurance Plus—
power follows the demand
of the load upon it

Sooner or later in life we all feel at the end of our resources. Whether young or old, man or woman, we begin to wonder if we can continue. Now and then a man sits down abruptly with himself and wonders if it is the time to quit, for we are living in an emergency period when people appear to be even more fragile and disposable in life's critical situations.

In this period of transiency of purpose and uncertainty of values, consider the spiritual grace of endurance as an assistance to you in refocusing your life. Your own private search for meaning in youth or age and your anxiety whether to quit or to persevere is not much different from the similar experience of the apostle Paul in his time. There is a recital of his adventures and tribulations in II Cor. 11:24-30, giving modern people a fuller background of appreciation of his spiritual discovery—that when he was weak, then he became strong.

We have come to an age of weakness through uncertainties, but in it we shall be able to discover our strength through spiritual endurance. The memory of our past strengths need not be the measure of our future capacities. When a man is weak, he discovers the greater depth of his own being, the wider horizon of his broader concern, and the unmeasured vertical of his concept of God's renewing power. Endurance is no different when one uses the term in the religious category than when one employs it in ordinary usage. Men who climb mountains know what endurance is. In the thin air of the mountains heroic endurance is no different from the banal endurance experienced in the heat and battle of private life, or the normal tensions of group living.

Over a dozen years ago a young Brooklynite named George Argus, Jr., and three others climbed to Mt. McKinley's pinnacle of over twenty thousand feet. They stood on the top to take pictures of their victory smiles. Argus said later that it was like visiting Coney Island. But it was no Coney Island experience on the eventful descent. Argus, who was the lead man, was cutting handholds as they came down a slick, razor-edged ridge of ice. The fourth man in the line of those roped together was a ranger named Thayer, who was an experienced mountaineer. All of a sudden, like a crack of doom, Thayer slipped on the ice and slid past the other three, dragging them all down a thousand feet. When they came to a crunching halt, Thayer was dead. Argus, Wood, and Viereck were alive. Argus had broken his leg. Wood and Viereck, unharmed, walked aside and agreed that they would have to leave Argus there alone and strike out for help. They made young Argus comfortable, and there he remained alone for almost a week.

Snow fell and covered his little tent with almost thirty inches. He said later when rescued, "I took the measure of every mountain peak in sight and tried to meditate about whatever I could see. I counted every day carefully and took what little food I could at regular hours. One day the snow fell on my woolen sock. I knew it would melt in the noon sunshine and then freeze at night. I spent one entire day moving my broken leg just to pull off one sock."

This kind of endurance learned on mountain slopes by a young Brooklyn man is typical of the same kind of spiritual endurance each of us is called upon to seek in all the areas of our lives. It is not only physical endurance that we need, but what one might call social endurance as well.

Many take for granted that modern human relationships are fragile. These may pass a man or woman through great tribulation, like Argus' experience on the mountain, with its pain, duress, and solitude. But as men and women go deeper to understand their own basic capacities to forgive and forego criticism, they will grow to understand the lasting spiritual goals of life and the art of getting along with other people. The reason we think we are living in a shallow age of conformity is that we are not willing to go down to the greater depths of personal discovery where we find our own measures of weakness and also discover our deeper measures of strength to appreciate the differences in other people.

Physical endurance in the mountains and social endurance in human adjustments are made of the same quality that we associate with spiritual endurance. The capacity of a person to endure is no different when he is on a mountainside hanging onto a cliff than it is when he is demonstrating courage and stamina in social relationships day by day. Endurance is no different when a person is creating fulfillment in his work, or working out a family relationship, or engaging in what seems like sharp and relentlessly unpleasant controversies of present-day religious and civic life. If one has any endurance at all, it is made of the same essence as that of Paul when he said, "When I am weak, I find my strength in God, because power comes at the point of need."

However, this kind of strength and endurance comes to

us in an area of personality that we often neglect. We are oriented to the emotions. We have certainly emphasized the intellectual and rational side of life. Some consider the question of the will to be out of vogue. It is legitimate to say that there is no distinction between emotion, intellect, and will, just as there is no separate distinction in the interaction of body, mind, and spirit. A person is an undivided essence of feeling, intellect, and will, all interacting at once. But we can emphasize the will since it is in that area of experience that we must train ourselves in the spiritual grace of endurance.

In the mountains climbers say that a hero is a man who goes one step farther. In the turmoil of big city living, in the restless mobility of the American way of life, the hero is also the man who goes one step farther. Is not this what Jesus said—"If anyone compels you to go one step, go one farther; if he says, give me your coat, give him your vest also"? When Peter countered with, "How often do I have to forgive?" Jesus said, "Top him one more! Seventy times seven in one day—forgive him." Jesus taught that personal endurance is a matter of plus one—one more step, one more day, one more breath, one more loyalty. That is the power of endurance to help one refocus a creative life.

I

Someone will ask at this point how one gains this endurance. There are several ways to deepen the power of endurance. One is to have a worthy goal. When a person places his thumbnail directly in front of his eye and blinks the other one shut, he cannot see anything. But as an artist does, when he holds his thumb and brush at arm's length, he can see all there is about him, as well as his hand. This he does in order to gain approximate dimensions and perspective. Likewise, when a person has a worthy goal, he has a larger view of all his life which he sees in relationship, but if he moves his extended hand's perspective back nearer and nearer to his eye, then fairly soon the nearness of the hand to the eye will blot out everything else, and he will see very little at all.

Today we live mostly on short-term projects rather than by long-term commitments. They are easily disposed of. They are often less rewarding than long-term goals, for a man is built, we learn from biblical knowledge, with a certain touch of eternity in him. It is when he has this long-term perspective of a goal in him that life makes more sense. It is in the long goal that a marriage makes sense, that a church relationship makes sense, that civic loyalty makes sense, that belonging to a religious body makes sense, that your whole endurance of a life career makes sense.

The disillusionment of the public generally with the war in Vietnam has been the haunting doubt whether the losses suffered have been worth it in the long run. Probably men and women have a suspicion that the sacrifice of all former wars was not really worth the cost. However, the struggles may have helped promote peace and perpetuate freedom. Yet the gains at so great a sacrifice cannot be kept vital unless the living commit themselves more diligently to the same long goal of constructive peace and social righteousness with justice, and see their efforts as related to those who were lost in battle.

II

A worthy goal gives a sense of priority. It also gives a sense of value. These all help one to endure a little longer since we all have more stimuli to handle today than we can use effectively.

If we are going to cope with the crosscurrents of life's pressures and stimuli, we need to be able to put some things aside as of lesser value in order to enhance the real things that count. In this respect we need to have a clear focus of our goals.

We need to have the ability, as does a ship, to close the doors into watertight compartments of buoyancy and preservation. We need to be able to shut out the engulfing sea and close in the buoyant hull of determined significance.

Many are familiar with the clanging bell which sounds on a cruising vessel when the bulkhead doors start to close and divide the ship into such buoyant watertight compartments. The importance of this safety device has been dramatized in the busy harbor of New York where ships have recently been sliced in half by collisions. One part has floated because of its sealed bulkhead doors, while the other has sunk.

Similarly, it is possible to have more personal endurance and consequent spiritual buoyancy by a focus that shuts out some things and shuts in the main purposes of life with respect to the worthy goal of doing God's will in daily circumstances.

This principle was observed again in a hospital corridor. The steel fireproof doors were held open with little thermal couplings in the chains. If the heat of fire should at any time reach the danger point, the thermal couplings would melt. Then the force of gravity would force the doors to close with a slam and place a wall of safety between people and the danger of fire.

With respect to refocusing one's life by clarifying one's goals, Dr. Paul Tournier of Switzerland said, "It is not enough for church people just to ask what is right and wrong. There is a higher level of life than that. It is to ask what is God's specific will for an individual alone to perform in his actions on any day." Within limits everybody knows right and wrong in general, but there is a higher level where God has specific instructions for individuals, given in little whispers, contacts, and nudges of guidance. When we are open to them, we can be his cooperators in service and deepen our endurance to fulfill them by the confirmation they give of his goodness to us.

III

Endurance comes when we have a worthy goal and when we keep a sharp focus of definition of our sense of values, but there is still another thing to help develop endurance. In the autobiographical notes in II Corinthians, Paul says, "When I am weak, then am I strong." There he is alluding to an experience you can verify in athletics or in other tests of tenacity. He declares that there are deeper capacities in all of us than we normally use. We call this facility second wind in distance running. There are many other records of the deeper capacity of human endurance. A Chinese sailor was hurled into the Atlantic Ocean when his ship was torpedoed off the coast of South Africa. He managed to salvage a small raft and drifted on it all alone for 133 days on the tossing sea. He was later picked up near Belem, Brazil. That was over four months of endurance of solitude, anxiety, and danger.

There is an even deeper capacity of mind, body, spirit, and love in the human frame than we all know. The wife of the founder of the Salvation Army said to her husband, "You cannot get to the deeper level until you have used up the ordinary capacity that you have." In other words, God doesn't give the extraordinary capacities until we have drained the ordinary ones. It is when we are weak, dry, empty, and ready to give up that we get our second wind. It is only in the draining of endurance that we discover our deeper capacities to become persons and to do greater service. When we have a hard job to do in life, in the home, at work, in the church, and in the conflict of urban problems, that is when we grow the most.

IV

There is greater leverage of service and spiritual relationship with other people than in isolated individual faithfulness.

109

If a person is to grow in his capacity to endure, he needs the example and encouragement of other people. We are particularly concerned for the transient people who have lived in communities for almost ten years, or more, and still have not affiliated with any congregation. They cannot usually go much deeper in their religious lives without some provision for testing or mutual association. They are living at a certain level of capacity, it is true, but it is only when they take on the concerns of a congregation with its many cares for other people, and with its loyalties to many worthwhile benevolent institutions, that they discover a second wind of spiritual service and grow by exertion and the challenge to a new level of endurance.

It would be much easier to be somewhere else than in a post of faithful service or worship. But it is in places of sacrificial duty that one tests the veracity of Paul's words that when one is weak, then one discovers strength. When one goes to the deeper levels of drained strength, one discovers the deeper levels of spiritual power. More than that, when one is weak or at the point of despair, one will more readily discover that one's renewed strength comes only from God.

We need other people to help us develop endurance, just as a solitary bee cannot produce honey. Honey must be produced in the corporate life of a hive or colony. It has been said by many that you cannot produce the deepest integrity of character and the endurance of human personality all alone. It must be done when one is in a vital relationship with other people, where there is trust and concern by other truth seekers. This is why we keep urging people to join some congregation. Friends who visit The Fifth Avenue Presbyterian Church in New York from Indianapolis or Indianola discover that the city congregation derives strength from their being there. The visitors also take something home with them from the strength they have seen in the congregation's confronting urban problems. Nobody can go it alone in life and keep up his endurance and depth in solitude. We need other people for inspiration and to help us endure.

V

Personal spiritual restoration on a daily basis is the way to gain endurance.

I saw a sign recently which I want to remember. In bold neon lights it stood out in the darkness stating, "Renewal comes through light, love, sleep, and change." When you walk in New York on any bright day, you can see people bathing their faces in the light of the sun's atomic furnace to restore their morale. But in addition to physical light, there is need of spiritual light, love which is expressed in concern, sleep which is physical rest, and change which is restored perspective. All these are needed to produce the renewal of endurance, just as they functioned for the prophet Elijah when he fought against the power of that irascible queen, Jezebel.

After his strenuous contest on Mount Carmel with her idolatrous agents, he felt exhausted, just as Jesus became exhausted by his spiritual conflict in the marketplace. Only Elijah said dejectedly, "Lord, I quit." But the Lord guided him to the healing stillness of a cave of refuge. There he learned that the power of life was not in the roar of the threatening wind, nor in the commanding stabs of flashing lightning. Rather, it was in the still voice of God within his heart telling him, "When you are weak, I will make you strong again."

VI

Many of us are perplexed by modern life. The confusion and complexity of existence increase and make it seem despairing. We appear to be living at a time when the seas of difficulty are coming over the ship's prow and sweeping the unsure from the deck. Sometimes it seems as if the wind has blown the chart out of the wheelhouse and we do not know where we are going. But as we read history we discover that it has always been this way in life—or at least that way for 150 years. Should we then ask for easier conditions of endurance than our fathers who suffered in order to build the significant spiritual and social institutions we share? Rather, let us take for granted that this is a new time of testing and refocusing and affirm with Paul the secret of personal endurance, "When I am weak, then am I strong." The present circumstances may be rough ones, but they probably are as normal as we shall experience.

When we are weakest, we discover God afresh rather than just our own selves. The point of our greatest controversial personal, social, political, or religious needs may be just the point where God will deepen our lives. Today may be the turning point in life as we seek to refocus it creatively in new channels. Let your imagination shine afresh on your job and see it in its new and deeper levels in the spirit of Christ. Turn the light of Christ's spirit on your personality and marriage and let it illumine new depths of understanding and companionship. Turn the light of Jesus Christ on your heartache, your anxiety, and suffering and see your deeper personal capacities develop through arduous endurance.

Basically, endurance is learned from association with other people as well as discovered by long-suffering private experience. When the renowned Daniel Poling's little son was operated on, he urged his father to stay with him all through the operation. When the anesthesia had been applied and his form was limp, the nurse suggested to the father that he might like to leave the operating room because it would not be a pleasant experience. With practical sagacity Dr. Poling thought he would just step outside and it would be easier for everyone. But as he turned to go and looked at his inert son, he decided to stay. At the end of the operation he was rewarded when the lad, struggling back into consciousness, painfully searched for his dad and said with cracked lips, "You stayed!"

Neither father nor son knew that there would be later a stormy night at sea when the same grown young man would be on the *Dorchester* when it was torpedoed. Hundreds of American boys then leaped into the cold water in one of the war's greatest tragedies. Four chaplains, including this son, gave their life belts to those who had none. Then with that staying power of endurance he had learned from his father, young Poling linked arms with the pastors of other faiths in their common hour of sacrifice. That is the secret of personal endurance—to know that when we are weakest, then God is our only strength to go on.

You will never know what you can bear until you have to actually do it—then the power comes.

The point of need is the place of power. The point of exhaustion is the place of renewal. The point of defeat is the place of rededication. The point of the end is the place to begin anew.

One More Step and You Are There—
the longest mile begins with one step

Living is a processional activity. It moves one step at a time
as one tries to bring life into clearer focus.

Two years after he had completed his term of office as the
sixth President of the United States, John Quincy Adams took
his seat in the House of Representatives. This is an unusual
step at any time, and it would still appear to be most unusual
in the light of today's cultural evaluations. John Quincy Adams
is remembered not so much for having been the President
and the son of the distinguished second President of the
republic, nor for his eminent career as a diplomat in France
and Russia, but for his devoted service as a working member
of the House of Representatives from 1831 until he died in
that building the day before Washington's birthday in 1848.

Before the ex-President left Quincy, Massachusetts, and
went back to Congress in the District of Columbia, people
said guardedly what they would say today, "It is just not
done. One does not become the President of the United States

and then go back to the lower hall of Congress. What will other people think?"

But Adams answered the silent opinion when he declared, "I have something to say to the people of the United States. I am not an abolitionist, but I do have a conscience and a love for my country. By the grace of God, as a member of the lower house, I shall do patiently what I can for liberty and justice."

Perhaps you may not be as familiar with this chapter of Adams' lustrous life. He was the one who, without ever being a political abolitionist, introduced resolutions which proposed that after the Fourth of July on a certain year every child born in the United States would be a free person. The gag rule of the House was introduced to stop him, and for years he was hounded, vilified, and voted down, as well as betrayed. Any one of us would have said, "I do not want to take this punishment any longer." But by the sheer lionlike qualities of his endurance, he took one more step each time toward the goal he had set. The integrity of this intrepid New Englander was able finally to command the respect of his colleagues and to break the gag rule. Eventually, he secured open debate about racial justice and helped further the cause of freedom of the slaves.

How can we regain such endurance in our lives when we face severe trials or when we seek to refocus our own lives or that of the nation? How can we regain the courage to contest principles and engage in honest debate among men who sincerely differ? How can we become the kind of persons who are as useful in present-day controversies as were the worthy men who established our republic? The answer is by remembering a significant principle in the Scriptures: Take one step at a time; take one more step in faith in God's providence until you persevere to the end.

Paul says it attractively, "Let us not be weary in well-doing:

116

for in due season we shall reap, if we faint not" (Gal. 6:9). I prefer the contemporary translation of J. B. Phillips which says, "In due season we shall reap if we don't throw in our hand."

In every man's life there is no time to quit. One more step at a time will carry him along even the most arduous trail. Whether you are thinking about your own personal need and grief, harassment, heartache, disappointment, disillusionment, or abject despair, you can still take one constructive step forward today. You may have a problem in your business, your home, or your society, where you do not see anything but brick walls ahead. But still there is this effective principle working with others in the dynamic creation of God so that to take one more step keeps you on the road toward your goal. To take one more step and then one more step again, in succession, works because this is a developing universe and not a static one.

Nothing in life is static—our lives, our health, our fortunes, our service, our institutions of government, education, and culture, for they all change upward or down. All are either rising in development or settling down into a plateau or sinking toward a decline. If we could ever master the concept that everything we are, have, and do is made up of one more step after another, then we could do what John Quincy Adams did. We could say that we have not yet reached the pinnacle of our lives just because we have been the sixth President of the United States. Rather, we have a longer furrow to plow in service in the lower legislative house where life is debated and influenced for the common good.

I read with interest how Howard and Ann Muir, from Trinity College in Hartford, took a bicycle built for two and pedaled the three thousand miles to the West Coast in seventy-five days. The thing that discouraged them the most was the forty flat tires, three in one day. (They came back by jet.)

117

On the way home they observed out loud that every married couple ought to do this trek together for greater endurance and more understanding of life/ All are tempted oftentimes to quit, but it is always too soon to quit because life is processional. It is made up of still one more step toward achievement, for in due season we shall reap the harvest of effort if we do not throw down our tools in despair.

It happens that this is being written on the exact date of the 162d anniversary of the founding of The Fifth Avenue Presbyterian Church in New York. In rereading its history I discovered that the questions which are being asked today are the very same which troubled the charter members in 1808. Some of the same inadequate answers are still being given to the same complex and dynamic challenges. But our forebears built the New York congregation because they took one more step in faith in the face of grave domestic troubles and international threats to peace.

When the War with Napoleon threatened chaos, when the Embargo Act wiped out the sea commerce of the city (the largest port at the time in the United States), they still built the church, because in dealing with the forces of life and society they had learned to take one more step forward even in days of adversity.

I

To apply this to our program of refocusing life, we need to realize that everything in life develops. Ours is not an "instant coffee" culture. Everything takes time to develop. For example, Thomas Edison laboriously worked out the incandescent light through thousands of repeated failures to get a filament to glow. Today you who enjoy the recorded stereophonic music of Tchaikovsky or Chopin need to remember what Edison also said later about his developing the phonograph, "I worked eighteen hours a day for seven months on one word—*specia*—and all I could get back was *pecia*." Imagine working eighteen hours a day for seven months just to get a sharp reproduction of one sound. Today your life is surrounded with beautiful music because of that effort. Have you attempted to demonstrate that same kind of stamina in your business, in your home, in your heartache, in your handicap, in your social problem, in your devotion to your city—to work tirelessly for seven months with no guarantee of success?

Men and women of all ages have always known that it took one more step after another to achieve results. Today, we all sing the praises of Jan Paderewski, the noted Polish citizen and musician, who died in 1941 in New York City. But have we forgotten that in his younger years when he tried to play the piano, people said abruptly, "You have stubby fingers. Try the cornet." He bought a cornet and went to a music master who said disconsolately, "You do not have the lip for it."

Finally, it was Anton Rubinstein who gave him a word of encouragement. "Young man, you might be able to play the piano. In fact, I think you can if you will practice seven hours a day." One word of praise and the patient taking of subsequent progressive steps earried Paderewski to his achievement.

It is always too soon to quit. It is too soon to quit life or the church or the city. All the problems and harassment which face life and institutions seem to confront every other situation as well, so why run to another problem without learning from what you have already invested where you are? It is too soon to quit most problems (but not all) because life is a constant development. There are surprise turns, changes, and breakthroughs.

Whenever you take sugar for tea or eat pineapple, remember a truth I learned in a preaching mission in Hawaii. It takes two years to grow sugar cane for the table. A pound of

119

sugar represents sugarcane that has lifted a ton of water out of the earth. Likewise, when you hastily drink pineapple juice in the morning, remember it also has taken two years to grow that delicious and sweet fruit. It takes two years of the burning sun and the sucking of the water and chemicals from the lava soil to make a pineapple. It is always too soon to quit, because if you faint not in your persistent efforts, in due season you shall reap, for everything in natural and social life is developmental.

II

Life is not only developmental, but it is also transformational. We live in a generation that unsuccessfully tries to make rigid black and white judgments. "It is this, or it is that," but life is not that way. It is only our laziness of thought that makes us want to say a quick yes or no. It is so much more convenient to categorize life, but that is not the way life is. Life is developmental and transformational; it is a process of stages like the metamorphosis of a caterpillar into a butterfly or of an adolescent into an adult, if he refocuses at every stage.

Look at the Dutch people, for example. Look at how our friends in the Netherlands have taken control of swamps and worked with farseeing vision and developmental engineering to drain them and make new land, extending like fingers out into the sea. Even after the obliterating damage of the last war, they have patiently gone back to reclaiming their hard work all over again, step by step.

The Irish also accomplished the same heroic task in ditching and draining their bogs to salvage pasture land. We often want everything served up to us whole and instantly, but nothing in life comes instantly, not even the dawn or the night, neither birth nor death. They come through development. More than that, life comes through transforming steps as when one takes a swamp, salvages land out of it, and grows a green meadow.

As you try to refocus your life, ask yourself candidly if you are a transforming agent in your place of employment, or are you just drawing a salary and complaining? Are you a contributing citizen in your community, or are you just another part of the problem? Are you a transforming agent working patiently step by step in some congregation, or are you just a free rider on other people's devotions? As someone in his sixties or seventies, or even in his twenties or thirties, are you a transforming person, or have you given up the hard struggle? Pause a moment and remember that in one more step ahead you may fulfill your efforts, because life is not only developmental, not only transformational, but it is fulfilling in the long run.

III

A farmer showed his son a large rock with a four-inch cleft. He said, "Son, I will show you how to split that rock. Throw in some shovelfuls of rich loam." Then he dropped in pumpkin seeds and covered them with more loam. "Watch," he said. "They will grow and split the rock by harvest time."

The son watched over the weeks as the energy of the germinating seeds developed into maturity and split the rock. Today we are not so patient. We want to go like Moses with a rod of anger and smite the rocky problems and cry, "Break open." But they do not break open that way. Sometimes we have to put in a seed and watch it germinate and grow to fullness before it splits the problem open. Often it takes more than one seed and more than one growing season.

Such stamina and perseverance are what Gandhi referred to as "courage without anger." We have lots of anger in today's turmoil. We have all we can use, but we lack that patient courage which transformed a restless and divided Indian population and made it a self-governing republic which has taken its responsible place in the commonwealth of nations. Think of the years of suffering that Gandhi went through, in the process of achieving this goal. Some might be embarrassed to be identified with Mahatma Gandhi's philosophy, but his courage is what is called for today—one more step of courage after another without anger, despite setbacks, in order to transform and develop a republic.

This same persistent plodding spirit is what the noted Harvard biologist, Louis Agassiz, taught his students before today's modern laboratories were built. "Look deeply," he declared, "and you will find truth in nature. You will be able to pull it out of its hiding." But we want to slap truth on life quickly. We seek easy panaceas for long-developing problems. Our social problems are inherent, so their answers must be indigenous. It takes time for a teeming city to reach its present stage of development and more time to grow even finer.

When The Fifth Avenue Presbyterian Church was founded, the area of its present location at Fifty-fifth Street was rural. Audubon, the distinguished bird lover and painter, had a twenty-acre farm up at what is now 155th Street. Today the area is all built up with apartment houses where it was once open space. Fifth Avenue Church's first minister, Dr. John Romeyn, came down from Albany because he thought the sea air would do him some good. He ought to be here now, when we say that we like to see the air we breathe!

I am trying to say what Paul wrote to the people in Turkey (then called Galatia). He wrote, "Don't throw in your hand and quit." It is always too soon to quit. Do not be weary in right doing or in doing any good, because everything has to develop, everything has to be transformed, and everything has to grow up. We tend to be too impatient with personal life as well as with larger public causes. This certainly is not a counsel for easygoing effort. Rather, it is an encouragement to persist when the forward motion seems slow.

IV

There is a time to sow and a time to reap, as well as a time to wait for the roots to grow. A beautiful example of this appeared in the newspaper account of the tremendous price bid for Velázquez's painting of the Moor by the Metropolitan Museum of Art in New York. The portrait of the Moor was really homework or a warm-up exercise to get ready for the real test. Velázquez had been commissioned to paint the portrait of Pope Innocent X. In order to do it with excellence and artistry, he summoned his servant, a mulatto of Moorish descent, and sat him down to paint his portrait as careful preparation for the main assignment.

This warm-up piece is now worth five million dollars. Velázquez might have rested on his reputation as a favorite of King Philip of Spain, for he was both the royal artist and a confidant of the king. Instead, he kept taking steps to improve his technique.

Velázquez did not know that his preliminary exercise would be worth five million dollars at auction when he warmed up for his dedicated work. Neither can we know that what we do today or tomorrow in some difficult situation, despite heartache or boredom, may prove to be the key to our whole life's puzzle. We cannot know until the venture is over.

A builder of fancy homes in a suburban development said to his chief carpenter. "Here is a project I want you to finish while I go to Europe. I want this house to be the best one we have ever done. It is a special situation."

The chief builder said to himself after his employer had gone away, "Why should I knock myself out for him? He has gone off to Europe for a vacation while I toil here. I have worked hard for him, but I have never gotten anything special out of it. Here is my chance to make something on the side."

So he used different gauge plywood and different grades of other materials. He made little cuts here and there in specifications in order to squeeze out money. Finally, he finished the house. Outwardly it looked as fine as it was intended. Then the owner returned and called the man into his office. He said, "You did a good job on that house. I did not tell you before, but that house is for you. You have been a faithful employee through all the years. I want you to have it as a gift for you and your family."

Today's cynical mood would probably say, "That will never happen to me," but the principle still works effectively for all. Do not be weary in doing good because in due season you shall reap if you faint not.

V

Hans Küng is one of the articulate evangelicals in the modern Catholic Church. It is possible that he might have been as great a leader as Martin Luther if he had lived in 1517. Recently he said most effectively what I am endeavoring to stress here—that there is a time to sow and to reap in the causes we are espousing. He declared, "It is not the task of the church to preach truth. It is the task of church people to be true." Truth changes its aspects. Fifth Avenue used to be a cow path. Today it is one of the world's glamorous avenues along with those in Paris and Vienna.

Everything changes. A man can be true in his spirit and not know that he has given an inadequate answer, but since he is true, he will change as soon as he discovers more truth. But another man can argue vehemently for truth and have his fingers crossed in deceit, or for vanity's sake remain unwilling to admit that he was wrong when confronted with new insights. Many persons fight and argue for truth with their fingers crossed in reservation or hold special interests as well as prideful misgivings at any necessity of admitting new or fuller truth.

Hans Küng said, essentially, "Don't be weary in well-doing. Be true and admit when you may be wrong. Ever change with the truth." The task of the church in the world is not to tell the truth or pound it into people, but rather to be true and to follow truth wherever it leads. That attitude alone will keep a person growing step by step all his years.

Finally, there is a time for everyone to go beyond himself step by step, beyond his familiar experience and caution. No man is ever fulfilled. A person senses his fulfillment only in the process of continual, fulfilling steps forward into the unknown and uncertain territory of the years. We never get to the point of total fulfillment in life. There is always one more step of love, courage, or faith to take. It is in striving and going toward the moving point that we find our feelings of achievement.

In Africa, David Livingstone once received a letter from a missionary society in England asking, "Have you found a good road to where you are going? We have some men who want to come and serve with you."

He scribbled back a message declaring. "I do not want the kind of men who wait until a road is built. Send me the kind of men who do not care whether there is a road or not."

That is the kind of men who built this nation and its institutions. Men of this type can remake modern America in the laborious task of moving one more step forward. John Quincy Adams was this kind of a man, one who did not wait for the road but who built the road himself by taking one step at a time toward justice for all.

The Matterhorn is 14,685 feet high on the Swiss side of the Alps. Edward Whymper, an English artist twenty-five years of age, came to sketch it and make wood carvings in 1865.

He tried six times to climb the slope and finally succeeded on the seventh attempt. He and his friends were the first to climb the Matterhorn from that approach, but on the return journey three of his companions were lost.

In a parabolic form this is the essence of the Christian life. Life is one more step toward the top and a costly journey even on the way down. In your personal life of sorrow, disappointment, or despair, you may have thought of ending your life or of giving up the struggle for both personal meaning and social adjustment. Try going on with God for one more step in faith. Go on just one more step forward in life today, for in due season you shall reap.

Take one more step forward in faith, knowing that God loves you as a person, that he cares for the concerns you yearn to see fulfilled, that he knows what efforts you have put into your life.

Take one step and a new focus may bring your life into sharp detail, "for we have to live with not knowing sometimes." *

---

* Christopher Fry, *A Yard of Sun* (London: Oxford University Press, 1970), p. 85.

IV. The Reward of Life
Is Commensurate with Its Risks

The Spiritual Law of Great Desire—
*   your deepest wishes motivate your will*

Persons tend to bring to pass what their imagination secretly envisions. "As a man thinketh in his heart, so is he," say the Scriptures, and this is a basic ground rule of life (Prov. 23:7). What a person saturates deep into his mind tends to realize itself in actuality. Hence there is a spiritual law which says that what you desire greatly tends to come to pass. Of course, there are limits and exceptions to this concept, as well as conditions and rules. However, it is a powerful enough device for you to consider as a legitimate tool in refocusing your life and bringing it creatively to a richer fulfillment.

One of the leading exponents of this biblical truth is Dr. Maxwell Maltz. He has written several volumes describing his discovery that the mental pictures of yourself and of life which you hold in your secret imagination tend to develop. He stumbled onto this important idea when he performed skillful operations of plastic surgery to make attractive faces for people who either had been born with malformations or had suffered severe damage in accidents. With most patients a new external face gave a great release of new hopefulness and purpose within, but other equally successful skin grafts produced no such spiritual exhilaration. It was then that Dr. Maltz realized that the inner personal picture of wholeness and mental approval had to match the outer one of beauty. Thus he formulated and tested the spiritual doctrine that the picture one holds of oneself and of life tends to become the reality of one's experience.

Intense thought influences the body. What is in the heart tends to become the action of the body. Few things are unpremeditated. Rather, they are more often the spontaneous eruption of prior deep meditation or internalized fantasy. A man has to see himself winning a race in order to run victoriously. A charming woman needs first to see herself as poised and graceful within her own mind. An effective salesman needs not only to believe in his product, but he also has to believe in himself and see a positive mental picture of his opportunity and capacity to fulfill his useful service.

In popular conversations over coffee we often hear people speak of "mind over matter" as if it were an unusual practice or uncommon resultant. The fact is that mind always works over matter leaving its imprint of confidence and courage, or taking its toll in inferiority and weakness. Thought influences action as well as the health of the tissues and the coordinated bodily processes which respond to intense desires or dislikes.

I

In order to practice the spiritual law of great desire, it is necessary first to read the biblical account of how it worked (Matt. 15:21-28). A woman of Canaan came to Jesus to seek his healing of her sick daughter. The Lord did not respond at first to this clamoring cry from the crowd. Later he told her he was sent chiefly to Israel and not to the Gentiles.

Rebuffed, the woman went again to the disciples asking them to intercede for her. They finally yielded to her insistent pressure and called her to Jesus' attention again. He spoke with her of the limitation of his ministry to the people of Israel. She retorted with deep desire for her daughter that even as the little dogs were allowed crumbs from the table, so he could do this favor for her, a foreign woman.

This insistent pressing of her claim caught hold of Jesus' responsive nature. He turned to her with full attention and approval. "Great is thy faith: be it unto thee even as thou wilt." And her daughter was made whole from that very hour.

This woman could easily have given up or have become discouraged. However, she seized every objection or excuse and wrenched it around to give her a new opening to seek the healing of her daughter. Her faith received the approbation of the Lord and became a model for modern disciples.

The law of spiritual desire is that you really have to want something to get it. The dream and desire must burn in your heart to be fulfilled. Halfway measures will not produce results, particularly in the last half of life when precedents and pressures have been fairly well accepted. It is only the most intense desire that will facilitate a refocused life in its renewed creative direction. Otherwise, there are too many popular excuses to coerce continued conformity and to cause one to accept the routine path.

It is amazing how electric is a practical spiritual principle, like this one, when it is cast from Scripture into the simple direct terms of secular life. It is equally amazing how people fail to see these same life-changing concepts in the biblical framework where they appear. The woman of Canaan is not just one isolated case. She is representative of the larger truth that great and intensive desires tend to come to pass. Human dreams and aspirations tend to come to pass only under the pressure of great desire, not under repetitious apathy or formal assent.

It would be well to pause here and observe that not all things greatly desired do come to pass just the way we wish them to do. Fairness prompts us to recognize both the validity of the principle and the limitations of its careless employment. My mind is vividly alive with the poignant memories of young sons and daughters whom loving parents earnestly wished to have lived to full life, but they could not be healed. Fairness warns us that we cannot have all we deeply desire even though intensive faith has more power than most of us employ in general usage. Moreover, we must assist one another in realizing that in the poignant situations above it was not the lack of faith or an incompleteness of desire that failed to fulfill the yearnings of parental hearts. It is a part of the human dilemma that great desires of faith do influence life, but not always nor automatically. And that paradox does not destroy the validity of using the principle to refocus life.

If you want to refocus your life in new and creative channels of service, attitudes, or approaches, then hold intensively before you the picture of what you greatly desire and it will come to pass more than in average ways, if not in its full scope.

There is even a positive residual gain derived from the persons and pictures we admire. They leave an influential imprint on us. Paintings and sculptures in the home work into the dreams of young people. A parent's or teacher's consistent character has its permanent effect and determination in another's life story.

II

That influence leads us to note another way to reinforce the deep desires of the heart. Keep people near you who share and reinforce your deep dreams. In the Bible story it was the insistent mother who supported the delirious yearnings for help by the sick daughter. It was the apostle Andrew who brought his brother Peter to the Lord, knowing of the deep religious hunger of his heart. It takes other people who share your hopes and dreams to bring them to pass, whether they be secular spiritual ones or religious practical ones.

The people with whom we associate daily have a great deal to do with developing or dampening our dreams and achievements. Nothing is more crucial in family life or in working associations than to support the deepest levels of godly desires in other people. The present mood of cynicism and diminishment is enough to destroy even the strongest. Few people have any estimate of how useful a ministry they could have in supporting the deep desires of those who seek something fundamental and special by faith in Christ—either healing of body or emotion, education or development of spirit, or more creative skills and new avenues of living. Unfortunately, we sometimes turn people away who lack the pertinacity to cry out over the heads of the indolent crowd, "Jesus, help me now!"

To be a person who supports and amplifies the deep signals of desire and the eager prayers of others is a ministry all in itself. It is a natural one to physicians and teachers, but it can become the glory of routine clerkships or of those on whom the world seems to have smiled with its material blessings, but concomitant price of boredom. Someone said that Jesus went about doing good, while most of us just go about. Here is a new ministry for men and women, well-favored or retired, to become skillful prayer partners to support the deep desires of those who cry insistently and alone at night, "God help me!"

It is practically impossible to know and do the will of God today in urban situations when one tries to go it alone. Each one needs the confirmation of another's friendship in Christ to know and to corroborate the will of God. More important, one needs the good fellowship of another who appreciates his Christian standards of work and play if he is to grow. Otherwise, the isolation of Christian ideals dwindles before the steady pressure and questioning of contemporary society. It takes two or three who love the Lord to keep alive the deeper desires of one person who seeks to refocus his life in middle passage or in later years.

III

It helps to bring deep desires to their fulfillment if one holds positive and affirmative pictures before his mind. Paul wrote to his friends in a Roman military garrison town, "Whatsoever things are true, whatsoever things are honest, whatsoever things are just, whatsoever things are pure, whatsoever things are lovely, whatsoever things are of good report; . . . think on these things" (Phil. 4:8). It is the positive good, the positive goal that draws a person onward.

Unfortunately, most of us have to remove a great deal of negative thinking from our minds. Positive pictures will do this much better than mental housecleaning or trying to sweep away the cobwebs of gloom. Putting a fresh flower in the room is the start of a subtle renewal campaign. Shining one's shoes will change a whole mental attitude of carelessness. A positive thought will overcome a dozen negative ones.

The difficulty for us today is that negativism is so easy and customary a style. We deal in negative, critical, and destructive terms all day long. They have a way of rubbing off onto our basic disposition. Then we assume the posture of defeat rather than the position of great desire. To refocus life, keep your inner spirit's desires alive by practicing positive affirmations and suggestions. Few people are strong enough to resist the slow cumulative lead poisoning of negativism. If you do not believe it, keep score for one day. Try to say one positive for each negative and watch the uneven trend develop.

The hypnotic effect of deep desires and attitudes can work either way—positively or negatively. The man who says he can, probably shall do it. The woman who sees her own side of loveliness and perhaps a single feature of charm is usually more radiant than a flawless beauty of anxious self-concern. The former hostess releases the inner beauty of all her guests, while the latter competes with the insecurity of her friends. Watch even the hardest-working office-cleaning woman smile and wipe her hands when someone takes the time to give her an affirmative word of recognition and praise. All the miracles were not completed in Galilee a long time ago. There are some left to be performed today in Gotham, or Goshen, or Great Bend.

It is possible to transform a person, a home, a school, or an institution by positive affirmation. Abraham Flexnor turned around the destiny of American medical schools in 1914 when he made a national survey with certain helpful recommendations. He had the courage to say the truth in a positive way. As a result we have the present high standards of the medical profession.

A sailor on a merchant marine vessel during the war changed the morale of his ship within three months by optimistic attitudes and affirmative action. His inner spirit drew isolated crew members into a fellowship which removed control of the ship's posture from a group of tyrannizing bullies.

One retired woman physician transformed the performance and inadequacy of a western state's Board of Health because she refocused her life in retirement on the joyful giving of positive assistance to others in achieving their creative desires for the community. When so many people are gripped by unsettling fears of injuring their careers or success, it falls to others to create the positive and courageous environment in which real progress can be developed without fears.

There are many things that retired people, who have felt

133

life's applause, can do for younger people when there is not likely to be any applause for leading the way, but certainly a few brickbats. This sort of encouragement to creative young people tends to be forgotten as an important creative outlet for older persons. It has great rewards, though, for both generations. It is not always the young who can take a chance involving their careers or their children; others who have experienced the vexation of life and its frequently shifting values can look death or defeat more squarely in the eye and risk a showdown with more than a likely chance to win because the spiritual law of great desire works for the person who knows what he wants under God.

Many people have no particular life plan. The early years come swiftly and automatically with their chores and tasks and advancements. But after the running and walking climb up the early hills, the mountains' last miles are often slow and painful, demanding a thoughtful strategy of carved handholds, carefully driven pinions, and deft rope work to scale the final summit. One can refocus his life to some sort of plan either to climb as far as he can, or perhaps a better way is to enable someone else to climb higher than himself because he has made the trail for others to follow.

For still other people their plan of life may be to live in the valley and forge well the strong irons and pikes for those who shall attempt to scale the icy peaks. Not all men should attempt the same things in life, nor should any man at all climb all alone without another's positive aid.

IV

Holding the higher plan of God up to one's own goals is another way to fulfill the deep desires of life. A man's plan for his life should not always be tailored to the available cloth. A life plan may not always be fulfilled in one generation. It may be so lofty a plan as to require two or more generations to work out the fulfillment of the grand design. To help accomplish this does not require one to be a slave to another's dream. Rather, it seeks only the voluntary inspiration to carry forward in one's own creative style the master foundations which another has built.

In fact, an easily obtainable plan of life is probably an inadequate plan. The appeal of Don Quixote and *The Man from La Mancha* is that the impossible dream does more for the soul and society than material goals reached overnight can ever achieve. Long perspectives have kept men and women alive in the despair of concentration camps where they lived like animals, near the death smell of human slaughterhouses. It takes a large-scale dream and a plan to nourish worn bodies and frazzled minds during such harassment. And is the worst of any modern city's secret ghettos much different in its effect on people than some ill-famed concentration camps were? Or is the comfortable boredom of a purposeless suburban life any less destructive than the city, despite its pleasant decor?

The envisioning of God's purposes for human life and modern times puts depth into personal plans for creative living. His intention of fulfilling human life for the city's diminished and discriminated people adds force to the worthy dreams of those who hope to fulfill their own aspirations now. Life's fulfillment lies not so much in search for oneself as it does in concern for the continuing kingdom of God, who has his own long-range, yearning desires for his children on earth.

Seeking to fulfill one's great desire by wishing for a thing is not the same as to will it into being. The spiritual law of great desire is a taxing one. It demands that every step of the way have such intense desire that it has to be willed into action over great resistances and objections. Few leaders even today bring to fulfillment their dreams and developments for mankind without suffering almost as much blind opposition and harassment as were characteristic of a more prejudicial period. Human nature has developed toughened resistances to change, as it has had to, so these reluctances test the worth of everyone's dreams and ambitious desires. As a result, no one can expect easily to receive his childish whims with their attendant dangers, as was the case with Finian's pot of gold and his reckless wishes. There is probably an upright cross, shadowing and testing each deep desire to purify it as well as the dreamer who seeks to bring it into reality by praying and willing each step of the process.

Usually the dream of great desire undergoes revision in the light of the cross as it gradually becomes clearer in definition. Part of the fulfilling process of desiring is to let the goal be modified until it becomes a conviction that unites all the inner resources of a person. The modified desire brings these forces into a sharp focus with all the aspects working together for God's good will.

No one could blame the family of Eddie Axelrod for being stunned when they were told by their physician that their teen-age boy would be crippled all his years and that these would be few in number. After a short period of depression and withdrawal, he seized upon the time remaining to organize a workshop in his bedroom. Using friends and neighbors to help him, he made felt cloth emblems and souvenirs. His sales of these creations to local variety stores increased, so that soon he hired many people to help him. As much as possible, he used people who suffered physical disabilities, just as he did. As a result, before he died a few years later, he had made Florida conscious of its privilege to hire the handicapped. One could not think that such a fine demonstration of human service was his initial boyhood goal, but it emerged over the few years of his courageous adjustment. As a permanent result, his sharply modified goals have continued to inspire the hiring of the handicapped all across the nation.

Too few of us capitalize on the tremendous power of right desires and the creative working force of worthy aspirations. We forget it is what we really seek in our hearts that comes to pass in life through our unconscious leanings and subtle preferences. We tend to go in the direction of our secret desires. We yield to them under surprise or pressure when we must make quick decisions or respond in emergencies.

How this works is partially seen in a new hobby which has appealed to many. During the summer holidays visitors to the old cathedrals of England secure permission to make brass rubbings of the beautifully etched plates and carvings of famous heroes and dignitaries of the past. The process is a fairly simple one of taping a full-length sheet of paper over the brass design. Then the artist rubs a stick of gold crayon over the black paper in rapid short strokes where he thinks there is a pattern or design. The crayon makes marks on the paper where the brass is below but not where the etched part has been cut away. As a result, the embossed effect is transferred to the paper. This process is like the drawing of a master plan in life. The relentless daily crayon effect of work and play moves over the blank sheet of the years, and the hidden design of the hidden desires and powerful imaginations starts to take shape and emerge in full beauty and transference.

Speaking in a Christian religious sense, one desires to let the design of Jesus emerge in the sketch of one's life, mistakes and all. He said, "I am come that they might have life, and that they might have it more abundantly" (John 10:10). "Whatsoever ye shall ask in prayer, believing, ye shall recieve" (Matt. 21:22). Such is the power of great desire, that what we imagine in the deep soul tends to emerge into actualized experience.

Renew Your Zest for Life at Any Age— let go and move forward

Refocusing life day by day sustains the zest of living. Familiar people and places tend to blur into a sameness over the years that obscures the constant action and interesting mutations. When this happens, boredom spreads over one's feelings, work, and home as mildew gathers in a poorly ventilated room. The soft powder of decay seems to settle on all the furniture of one's existence until he begins to think it might be an inevitable part of life. But just as fresh air, sunlight, and circulation can drive away the dampness of a room, so can positive changes keep the spirit of defeat from settling down on the unceasing struggle for creative existence.

The increasing pressure of the years causes some to settle it in terms of a silent agnosticism. They question the worth of earlier battles they fought with gallantry, and now they avoid new conflicts with a caution that does not express the deeper desires of their hearts. Others facing the same conditions try to bluff their way through them with a caustic cynicism which becomes more biting with the years and drives away the friends who used to balance it with their conviviality. In either approach the terms of life remain the same and require a renewal of enthusiasm to cope with conflict and change.

The youthful years face the same hard demand for a renewal of zest, although there are sufficient varied challenges that the insistent need for restoration may be hidden. Nevertheless, the principle of the plateau and the flattening out of excitement recurs in all ages, even if it is noticed more sharply in retirement or just before then. Therefore, learning how to renew one's spirit and vitality of approach is a recycling task to be mastered early in the years, not just in the last ones.

William James, the great American philosopher of pragmatism, went through an upheaval in his career. For about two years he suffered acutely from what has been called a nervous breakdown. Of that harrowing experience he wrote later that he clung to one thing, his faith in God, and derived comfort from believing that underneath are the everlasting arms of God. Like the psalmist he felt himself slip in the miry clay of despair, but then he regained his footing on a rock.

The experience of boredom, defeat, despair, and the recovery from it is more usual than most people care to admit. At least it is prevalent in minor degrees at some time in each life. The Bible recounts how it happened to such heroes as Abraham, Elijah, John the Baptist, and Paul.

The need to restore zest and a sense of direction in the contemporary mood of turbulence is apparent to such a distinguished scientist as Werner Heissenberg, who wrote *The Faith of a Modern Physicist*. He declared that in the midst of relativism you can keep your orientation by faith. This is what Paul did in renewing his faith. He said, "Forgetting those things which are behind, and reaching forth unto those things which are before, I press toward the mark for the prize of the high calling of God in Christ Jesus" (Phil 3:

13-14). At least one can have inner stability during a time of upheaval.

Roger Bacon said that there were only three ways of knowing life—by authority, by reason, and by experience. The last way, he pointed out, is the best one. Experience is the key to renewing zest at all stages of life. The usual cultural pattern is to be educated and configured by other people's opinions and reasons. As a result, one's own outlook becomes formal, verbal, and conceptual. It loses the tang of veracity and the excitement of personal participation.

Experience, on the other hand, is a probing, testing, and searching out of constantly changing situations. It involves the whole person in complete engagement with the interplay of circumstances. The person becomes alive in the struggle. He has to for his own self-preservation and safety. He both learns from his environment and interacts with it during the process. Life assumes more of its intended role of action and passion in the course. Oliver Wendell Holmes, Jr., said that if a man did not share the action and passion of his times, it might be said of him that he never lived.

I

Life itself is operational and experiential. Here is the place to begin the process of sustaining interest over boredom and renewing zest over apathy. This involves a switch from a word orientation to an action viewpoint. Another way of achieving this posture is to realize that a word is only a symbol of an action or thing which one can reduplicate. The word is nothing in itself. Words are only shorthand terms standing for creative operational experiences. As such, the words are like dried soup crystals which have to be brought back to steaming flavor and aroma by pouring boiling water on them.

Language itself recognizes the difference between words

of formal, static terminology and words of sweat, toil, and involvement. The French use *savoir,* meaning to know with the head, but they describe *connaître* as to know with the heart's own experience.

In the Orient one language uses *smriti* to mean, "I know because someone told me," and *sruti* to indicate, "Yes, I know because I was there."

The Reformation fathers employed two words for the vital word "faith." They used the Latin *fides* for faith that had become a code or formal written creed. They used the word *fiducia* for a living faith of experience because it represented one's own personal trust and involvement with God. You can catch the impact of it in the New Testament where an agonizing father cried, "Lord, I believe, help my unbelief." Here he acknowledged his creedal familiarity and correctness but aspired with Jesus' help to venture into the deeper risks of uncertainty in order to gain healing for his child. Many modern church people feel the same way. They subscribe to a faith correctly but without any zest. They yearn for the daring to move closer to God in uncataloged spiritual experiences in their own lives.

It was this way in earlier times too. All religion was then adventurous living. It had not yet been encoded, with the implicit demand that one subscribe to the code rather than to the validating experiences. In fact, there is no one word for God in the Old Testament. Their experiences of the lordship of God were so precious to the ancients that they used a new form of an old word, *Adonai,* to convey it. The word symbol stands for the action experience of God, who was known by many different names in many varying aspects. He was called the God of power and life. He was El Shaddai, the Almighty who accomplished good purposes in people's lives. He was the compassionate one whom lonely Hagar called "a God who sees me."

Unfortunately, modern man calls God only by the technical name of his native tongue. Allah, Dieu, or Gott. He may believe in the technical term, as he is supposed to by community pressure, but he may never have experienced God in his own way. Here is the place to renew zest and refocus life. Any man's word for God is only one Brownie camera's snapshot of one instant of God's interaction with a man or a woman, or both, in a given moment of history. At best, the picture is a flat one, a glimpse of Someone who can be experienced afresh all the years of one's life with consequent enthusiasm if one dares to probe toward the ultimate—beyond the neat fences and hedges of protective creeds and codes toward what they stand for in impressive experiences of God.

In the creative years of religious periods men do not master words and phrases, rather they experience God in action as did Paul when he left the strictures of Pharisaism for the adventure of following Christ in all of daily life among the Gentiles. He was blinded. He was healed. He was forgiven. He was guided. He was rebuked. He suffered. He was chastened. He was rewarded. He was arrested and imprisoned. In all these experiences he was writing, "I know whom I have believed, and am persuaded that he is able to keep that which I have committed unto him against that day" (II Tim. 1:12).

The way to renew zest is to exchange received truth into experienced truth and to know how the conversion process works in order to keep on changing ideas and symbols into actual exhilarating, motivating knowledge.

Words are like keys to a safe deposit box. They open the way to the treasure. They are not the valuables themselves. Even the treasures in the box may be a symbol just as a negotiable bond represents industrial real estate, tools, and machinery. One can play with keys, bonds, or religious words until boredom comes, but zest returns in the experiencing of

143

machinery humming into production and in the awareness of other lives fulfilling themselves in rewarding work. It is one thing to talk about a mission. It is another to do a mission. Zest is an aspect of functioning, not a function of feeling.

II

Zest follows participation and involvement in the risk of some particular aspect of living. Enthusiasm returns from experiences which verify the verbal reports of another's creative endeavor. To turn words back into events is to generate vitality. Forgiveness, for example, is a word concept, but to forgive another wholeheartedly, face to face, is to recapture joy sufficient to motivate still more productive participation. Take the word "sacrifice" as a religious shorthand expression. It is a cold term until a father experiences the light in his child's eyes and even forgets what he gave up for his child's education and development. The rate of return is so great that it could hardly be called a sacrifice in strict definition.

Faith is another general word with a variety of meanings which loses its force as a strict term. It is more of a dynamic word of risk and action. Faith means a validating process involving participation and commitment. It is something like hand cranking an antique Ford engine. Faith cannot guarantee that it will start, but neither will it start at all without the cranking action in faith. Faith is a sort of preliminary work that leads to fulfillment.

Faith is a way to be more nearly right in a world where nothing is ever wholly right. Faith will not lessen your burden or foresee all your future, but it will give you confidence and strength to keep on engaging life and growing in the process. The Bible declares, "Faith is the substance of things hoped for, the evidence of things not seen" (Heb. 11:1). Faith is demonstrated by actions in specific situations and not merely by general assent to the word. Faith is the venture of a person who is obedient to a situation where he can expect God to act too. More tersely stated, it is Abraham going out from his homeland in obedience to God's call, not knowing exactly where he was going.

III

Zest, then, is the result of action and experience-centered living, rather than the futile attempt to sustain a feeling by words, codes, and formal creeds.

More than that, zest is the dividend of involvement in the process of verifying the experience of God by others in terms of one's own community and culture. By his own experimentation, one can add to the experienced truth of others. No one can be totally right. New insights emerge where several partial views meet. Most people see through a glass darkly, according to Paul. The authority of truth is not just the weight of fact and argument alone, but the wholehearted acceptance and perception of insight into an action. Probably there is right now more truth approved and waiting at hand, but stubbornly resisted, than there is truth that has been already attempted and confirmed by trial. One only cries "Eureka!" when he discovers it afresh for himself. As an aside, you never hear a tither debating about the practice of systematic stewardship. He gives and therefore he knows. You rarely hear a lover philosophizing about affection. He loves and therefore he knows. A man of faith does not speculate. He specifies.

IV

At this point some modifications need to be introduced to the line of thought. Activism is not all there is to life. There is reflection and meditation, too, but reflection is not a contradiction of the premise that participative experience leads to enthusiasm. Obviously, there has to be a balance. Even more important is the task of maintaining the relationships that make creative involvement possible. The relationships are active, changing, straining, and restored. The idea becomes highly graphic when one watches a fragile reconnaissance plane nuzzling fuel from a cumbersome air transport tanker in mid-flight. The approach is cautious and tentative. The connection can be broken and resumed. The air may be too turbulent for the exchange of fuel at all. This vital picture is a more accurate one for the old word "righteousness," often misread as if it were a blueprinted rectitude with no consideration of constantly changing factors in the human scene.

Zest returns to life when one sees the maintenance of the shifting relationships as a primary task. The bearded son with his insistence on personal liberty is not in a permanent condition. The frightened arbitrary mother is not in her continuous role. The fast-talking operator of a get-rich scheme or the demure man or woman who seems to have escaped all conflicts are not in their lasting conditions. They change, rapidly and cataclysmically, for better or for worse. Relating to the new situation is always the new challenge with its self-rewarding zest or the humiliating admission that one has ceased to grow.

V

To keep flexible to the changes in one's own lot as well as in the lives of others, there are daily exercises to accomplish in the process of regenerating enthusiasm.

It takes considerable effort to look for opportunities to live for the sake of others, although they are plentiful about us. The normal instinct is for self-advantage, but the reward comes mostly in considering and supporting the struggles of other people. Assisting their needs becomes the stimulation and opportunity for self-expression and personal renewal.

To affirm one's own individual humanity on a deeper level every day is an exciting or frightening practice. It depends on how you look at it and how human you dare to be. Imagine the interplay when a supervisor has laid down the law severely to his group and has pointed out the mistakes of others caustically. He suddenly discovers at his own desk that he too has made a careless error. He can save his own face by ignoring it, although he is aware that his group also has noticed his mistake. Or he can try a new depth of religious experience. He can share his humanity in open acknowledgment with the others and trust them. He will not be naïve enough, however, to expect everyone to understand, but he may make life more tolerable for one, and he himself will grow rather than fossilize. Too often the safe and expected norm of response becomes the shallow measure of creative action and also its grave.

To innovate with life and to experiment with God's up-to-date operations is both daring and costly, and equally rewarding. For centuries men and women drove away to the caves those who were demented or unbalanced. The rejection and isolation only added to the emotional deterioration of the victims. Some communities even chained their outcasts. However, one courageous Frenchman, Philippe Pinel, saw a more humane treatment of the insane as a path to their restoration. Suiting action to his careful reflections, he unchained his charges and saw them respond to freedom and loving nursing care. This was the first step toward accepted modern standards of mental hygiene and therapy. But he was vilified and suspected for his efforts, which took some time to validate themselves in public opinion.

Whatever progress is to be made in contemporary social and cultural life, whatever gains are to be made for world peace and racial equality, are going to be as costly today. It is wishful thinking to expect radical changes among people for any less expenditure of courage. And the reward of enthusiasm and returning zest is just as great for the participants as is the resultant bondage of apathy and boredom for those who choose to escape involvement in life's creative process.

Probing the fringes of life is a way to find the growing edge. Questioning the world's axioms is one way of locating God's basic principles and separating their distortions. Older men and women are often in a position to assume more of these risks than young people, whom the world generally thinks of bearing the cost of adventure and daring. A retired college president assumed the back-breaking work of re-establishing an institution of professional training, and succeeded. He had much to give and little to ask for himself. He could afford to probe the newer horizons of that healing profession and question or drop some archaic methods and outlooks. The hornets of animosity raged about his head, but the calm eyes of seventy-plus years watched his tormentors tire of their irritation and begrudgingly acknowledge his creativity. Is it needful to add that the older man renewed his zest daily? He went on to face similar impossible challenges which were not yet ready to provide adequate support for a younger man needing the encouragement of status, good press releases, and the tendered badges of achievement. There is a season for both stages, but it requires wisdom to know when one period turns to the other, just as a good sailor senses when the wind has shifted in the night.

To innovate, to probe, to involve, and to affirm are all legitimate ways of verifying God's goodness over the years in actual human experiences, with consequent renewal of personal enthusiasm.

But an even more exciting way to move ahead during the years is to anticipate one's own new birth every day, as well as that of all others. People wake up new and fresh but quickly fall back into old patterns or expectancies before they can climb out of their defensive trenches of conformity to meet the new day.

The changes of each new day will be subtle, as is the dawn.

They can accumulate, as does the burning of noontime heat. They can be abrupt, as nightfall comes with its chill, often unnoticed. To encourage the daily growth is to engrave it deeper and to support it steadily while it is still tender and fragile. To ratify the growth of another person is to nourish one's own.

The half has not been told of any life, not even the greatest. The best part of one's years is the freshborn "today" in everyone. God provides in each day's task the renewal of zest and inspiration to see it through twenty-four hours. The treasure lies hidden near at hand under some obscure covering, waiting to be discovered by the seeker who believes the divine promise that there is sufficient enthusiasm for every day's demand through all the years. This was Robert Frost's implication when he wrote:

> I shall be telling this with a sigh
> Somewhere ages and ages hence:
> Two roads diverged in a wood, and I—
> I took the one less traveled by,
> And that has made all the difference.*

---

* From *The Road Not Taken* from *The Poetry Of Robert Frost* edited by Edward Connery Lathem. Copyright 1916, © 1969 by Holt, Rinehart and Winston, Inc. Copyright 1944 by Robert Frost. Reprinted by permission of Holt, Rinehart and Winston, Inc.

149

You Can Win Life's Battle—
in the search for meaning and fulfillment

Of course, that is the main question: Can you win life's battle? Or do chance and misfortune in this speedy technological age make it unreasonable to hope for personal fulfillment? Then there is also the question of the relation of Christian faith and its promises of God's care, as well as the aspects of the struggle for existence under modern conditions of war and social upheaval. The answer to this paradox and frustration underlies every person's whole existence in his work, play, or prayer, whether he can admit it or not. Someone asked Robert Frost, "Do you find much meaning in life?"

He replied, "Some days yes, and some days no."

Martha Duffy said of him that he wrote from a sure and deep humanity. His knowledge of evil was subtle and real. So was his natural grasp of people and their sorrows. That is why there is no rhetoric in Frost, no passionate effusions or rampages. He knew life was a struggle and a suffering from experience. His wife of forty-three years refused to admit him into her room as she lay dying, though he sought desperately to receive her blessing and forgiveness.

It helps in the struggle to win life's battle if you know it is a battle to the end—and not always a fair one at that. Some people in childish immaturity hope resolutely for a day when there will be no more struggle on earth, but if there is any lesson to be learned from the spiritual giants in the Bible, it is that life is a continuing battle and a struggle to the very end.

This is not quite so bad as it sounds, for struggle is basic to life. If there were no people on the earth, the planet would still be the scene of struggles to maintain itself through summer and winter, day and night, with their physical tensions of heat and cold, light and darkness. The whirling orb itself exists in a tension with other celestial counterpressures engaged in a gravitational struggle with each other.

Man's life is a struggle of working and resting. The tension continues inside his mind as well as in his muscular interplay of forces. Plato noted that the white horse of virtue struggled in the harness with the black horse of passion as man, the charioteer, tried to control both forces. So the psychic nature of man becomes a battle for meaning within himself as well as a struggle for physical existence.

If life is a struggle to reduce or overcome tension and animosity, it is also a great part of wisdom to learn how to cope with those forces that cannot be eliminated. The normal life will need to learn over the years how to overcome each day's burden despite rapid changes, continuing conflicts, enervating depressions, and unreasoned calamity that strikes without warning.

In 1963 Patricia Neal, the talented actress, won an Oscar for her role in *Hud* and thoroughly enjoyed the recognition it brought her. But one day in the early months of her pregnancy, following this pinnacle of acclaim, she suffered a severe stroke. She did not know what had struck her. She could not talk. She could not walk. She could not read or write. She could do nothing.

Her children, puzzled by her incapacity and inability to respond, turned to their nanny for love and security. Their seeming rejection of her only added to her heartache. Drawing heavily on her faith, she struggled courageously to relearn how to walk, to write, to frame with the delicacy of her lips the words that stood for love. Eventually she recovered and starred again in the film *The Subject Was Roses.*

More than is known or recognized, most men and women of fame or frailty must manage to secure whatever victories and meanings they can in life through a continuous struggle with great forces and odds.

Catherine Marshall is another contemporary example of one who faced life's breaking point and gained deeper insights in the struggle. She has written out of her own experiences of illness and sorrow of her search for meaning and her later fulfillment in her family.

I

The prophet Elijah was a man close to God and the ferment of his times. One would think that he should have had a way to fulfill his life without a struggle. Actually, it was in the struggling that he found himself and renewed his spiritual insights, rather than that his religious views protected him from the battle of existence.

When things were worst, God instructed Elijah to hide out in the mountains where he could feed him and provide a brook of water. The ironic situation is that the brook dried up after a while. (I Kings 17:6-7.) Then God led him to a new refuge in the guest room of a widow's home in Zarephath.

God has alternative routes for people. He is not boxed into one scheme. Brooks do dry up. Jobs change. Industries are replaced by new products. Products disappear from popular demand. Years of physical powers diminish sometimes even to a standstill. Yet God can be faithful to help people win the battle of life in their particular circumstances.

Changes come for better and for worse. Some are only temporary or provisional, as when a cofferdam diverts a river and permits bridge foundations to be sunk into the riverbed. Change and changes are part of the struggle, and learning to cope with their mingled tensions and benefits is a better strategy of winning than trying to stop the changes altogether.

II

While changes may be irritating, and most of them appear to be so at first, they are not the main element in the battle of life. Changes can be beneficial and stimulative as well. But there is also the element of conflict in life besides changes —a combat of personal powers and perversity of will. There is a built-in opposition in life, which Paul described as a wrestling against principalities and powers, not just flesh and blood. Elijah was confronted by a persistent antagonist in King Ahab and his revengeful queen, Jezebel. Both these enemies made the prophet despair for his life and become despondent over God's care for him. But such political struggle is part of all life in every generation and climate. It begins between children in the nursery. It extends even to power struggles near the foot of Jesus' cross, where fellow disciples compete for favored places at the Master's feet.

One cannot ignore the pressures and issues of his own life and his times. He may have to stand up to greed or evil or apathy and its dinner-jacketed companion of respectability. He may have to risk loss of fortune or even death itself on some Mount Carmel in a struggle with a modern priest of Baal, as did Elijah. Even the boldness of his confrontation is not enough to secure victory in life. The moment after an achievement is gained, the negative forces polarize at still another point and the battle is resumed. This takes spiritual endurance, especially when an issue may not be resolved in one's own lifetime. It may even get worse, because one has stood his ground, before it is concluded satisfactorily.

III

Even the prophet Elijah wilted under the unrelenting pressure of conflict and change. He cried out in despondency, which followed exhaustion in the struggle, "God, I wish I were dead." Even the most religious of lives is not always a pretty one. Other prophets and modern saints besides Elijah have experienced agonizing doubts and despair. The God they served seemed absent or preoccupied. It was at this point of almost suicidal defeat that Elijah found his renewal in rest, solitude, food, and a restored vision of his useful role in the continuing struggle.

The centuries since have not changed the nature of the human crisis or the formula for its recovery of strength.

Lili Kraus is a distinguished Austrian pianist who lives now in Rochester, Minnesota, with her daughter and son-in-law. In 1942 she and her husband fled from the German occupation of Austria to Java. There she was no safer. At first, as a European, she had some freedom under Japanese occupation to play concerts at the concentration camp. She would carry letters from husbands to wives who were detained in separate compounds and provide what little money she had to buy small supplies at camp stores as a humane service.

Suddenly, however, she was accused of being a counter-agent and of carrying secret weapons for insurrection. She was seized and placed in a tunnel with three other women who crouched in a space four feet in diameter and twelve feet long. The others, whom she knew, admitted to her that

155

they had aided insurrection. "But Lili," they said, "we know you have not done anything to be incriminated."

Yet the commandant of the camp interrogated, pressured, and harassed Lili Kraus to make her confess. "Tell me all, and I will let you go," he promised.

"But I have done nothing!" she avowed.

One day during the interrogation, she noticed a piano in the room beyond the officer. He caught her glance at it and stubbornly commanded, "Play it." Although she had been forced to scrub latrines and had damaged her hands, she prayed, "O God, give me the strength to play!" For half an hour she was permitted to play without interruption.

Then he barked, "Stop! If you will tell me what I want to know, you can play some more."

"I have nothing to tell you," she cried as she was ushered back to her confinement.

As she stumbled along, she thought she noticed the sentries' rifles were more relaxed in their arms, that prisoners working outside the office were less agitated, that there was less strife at the evening mealtime lineup.

After a week of quiet, she was summoned back to the commandant's office. She felt great anguish and prayed for strength to face the ordeal of further questioning and threats.

Instead of a harangue, the officer said curtly, "You will be brought here one afternoon each week to play the piano."

There was no chapel in the camp and no religious service. Lili Kraus became the minister to everyone's spirit by her music as she struggled along with the others in the battle for existence under duress. Her weekly piano playing became a ministry of mercy to those in desperation, who before had felt it was better to die than to try to live in that hellhole. She is still ministering with her music in today's anguish and social struggle in American cities.

Even in the bleakest situations and in the most unusual

circumstances man can still find God's provision for release and renewal from his exhaustion, defeat, and depression. In prison camps or their counterparts, on crosses of destruction, defamation, or denial, God reaches out with spiritual renewal to those who by necessity or endeavor probe the depths of life around them while they cry, "Let me die," or "My God, why hast thou forsaken me?"

IV

The ordeal of change, the tension of conflict, and the gloom of depression are not the worst of life or all that can define the battle for life's meaning. There is also calamity—unexpected and unreasoned. The Bible describes it as the arrow that flieth by day or the pestilence that walks stealthily in darkness (Ps. 91). It is what happened to ancient Naomi, who fled a famine in Bethlehem with her husband and two sons. These three men died, however, and were buried in alien soil at Moab. Only her daughter-in-law Ruth returned with her to Bethlehem. But the two women recovered from their sorrow by trustful action and fortitude of spirit as they refocused their lives for a second start.

Calamity seems more real in a modern situation. A young married man in the church had learned to offset the complete paralysis of his legs that polio had produced. He was agile on crutches held with strong arms that also controlled all the levers in his automobile. His keen brain channeled all his energy into his talented leadership in the expanding computer business of which he was the president.

No one really saw what happened to him one day. They only heard it, where he seemed to be nimbly deplaning from a transcontinental flight on business. There was a sharp cry, the rattle of sliding crutches, and the murmur from his ashen face revealing the torture of his fractures as he lay crumpled on the concrete apron at the base of the stairs.

Already acquainted with despair, he was settling down waiting for frail bones to knit and running his business from a bed, when a visitor informed him that the corporation had been bought out by a larger firm which would not need his services.

If there is any rock bottom in the struggle of life, he yearned to touch it then with his motionless toes as depression blanketed his mood. However, he found his bottom of despair and slowly, doggedly claimed God's promise, "I will never leave thee, nor forsake thee" (Heb. 13:5). Today he is still struggling with crutches, heartache, and the present economy, but he is courageous, cheerful, and providing for his family.

V

The critical question is: Can a person refocus his life from year to year during his life-span and fulfill it? Can he make a spiritual comeback from unforeseen radical changes, from consequences of unfair conflict, from the entanglement of mental depression, and from the stinging blows of physical and financial calamities? Some demur with Shakespeare that life is a sound and fury, just an unaltering, unvarying pathway to nil—a stalemate of dust and desire. Others feel, as Thomas Hardy wrote in *Tess of the D'Urbervilles,* that man is caught in a mechanical fate which he cannot escape, nor need he try.

Thornton Wilder wrestled with the same theme in *The Eighth Day.* For him, the eighth day was the one of recreation after God rested the seventh day in the creation cycle. He indicated that this is a time of hope and renewal in the struggle for fulfillment of life, even though there will always be a conflict. But it can be a meaningful and satisfying one even when not always fulfilled by man's materialistic standards or his mythical aspirations after worldly success and reputation.

Teilhard de Chardin wrote of the human encounter that

158

it moves toward the Omega point (this being the final letter in the Greek alphabet and the symbol of God's final goal). He believed that God has a purpose of design. Man's endeavor is to move through his days of joy or nights of terror toward that fulfillment.

In a sense every day is a new beginning in the process. The day's challenge is a valid part of the struggle. Even though one is fulfilling only a part of a small subsystem of life, he is contributing to it. This was the message about the public school teacher in the film *Up the Down Staircase*. This also is the hope for novices who see dreary years of struggle ahead. It is also the encouragement for those whose golden days of career achievement are behind them. The meanings of those days and the measures of those years of service are entwined into a whole fabric by the Designer.

VI

Basically, the struggle to fulfill life's meaning is an effort to fulfill it outside one's own self in terms of God's larger will for society. To be truly himself, a person needs a sharp focus outside himself. Otherwise, an unhealthy subjectivism or self-preoccupation will seek meaning in unrewarding areas such as drugs, sex, honorary badges, and prideful distinctions, or in a never-satisfied drive of ambition and restless striving. Jean Cocteau, honored by the French Academy before he died at the age of seventy-four, said, "All my life I carried an ill-suited assortment of cargo, and I spent so much time worrying that I never lived."

The fundamental focus of life is that God's will is to be fulfilled through human actions and responses to him, despite the ill-suited circumstances. When God is put first and as the main focus of life, the human scene takes on a different interpretation, since all life's circumstances are interpreted ones, translated from a major point of view either of God or of

159

self. When we diminish our selfishness, we also decrease our helplessness in life. When we give life and support to others, we fulfill ourselves as well as the kingdom of God's love.

Wernher von Braun, one of the chief scientists of the space program, made a significant comment: "Today, more than ever, our survival depends on adherence to spiritual principles. Science has found that nothing can disappear without a trace. Nature does not know extinction. All it knows is transformation. If God applies this fundamental principle to the most minute and insignificant parts of his universe, does it not make sense to assume that he applies it also to the masterpiece of his creation—the human soul? I think it does. And everything science has taught me—and continues to teach me—strengthens my belief in the continuity of our spiritual existence after death. Nothing disappears without a trace."

The meaning and the intensity of the valid struggle to refocus life year by year in the spirit of Jesus Christ are described succinctly by T. S. Eliot:

> For us, there is only the trying. . . .
> Home is where one starts from.
> As we grow older
> The world becomes stranger,
> The pattern more complicated.*

Yet from the blindness of noontime or the shadows of evening comes the voice of one who also struggled through all his years to find his meaningful existence in doing God's will on earth: "In the world ye shall have tribulation: but be of good cheer; I have overcome the world" (John 15:33). "Lo, I am with you alway, even unto the end of the world" (Matt. 28:20).

---

* From "East Coker," *Four Quartets,* in *Collected Poems 1900-1962.* By permission of Harcourt Brace Jovanovich and Faber and Faber Ltd.